The Guns N' Roses Worker-Traveller

Marc Latham

chipmunkapublishing
the mental health publisher

Marc Latham

All rights reserved, no part of this publication may be reproduced by any means, electronic, mechanical photocopying, documentary, film or in any other format without prior written permission of the publisher.

>Published by
>Chipmunkapublishing
>PO Box 6872
>Brentwood
>Essex CM13 1ZT
>United Kingdom

http://www.chipmunkapublishing.com

Copyright © Marc Latham 2011

Edited by Keziah Poole

Chipmunkapublishing gratefully acknowledge the support of Arts Council England.

The Guns N' Roses Worker-Traveller

Introduction

Music can be your companion for all moods. While I now listen to a variety of music, in the 1980s I was serious about my rock music; it was like a religion to me. I therefore didn't buy music outside of the rock genre. Fleetwood Mac was there when I was mellow; Pink Floyd when I was feeling down and alienated; and Metallica or Megadeth when I was manic.

In 1987 Guns N' Roses released *Appetite for Destruction* and I was the first to buy and promote it amongst my friends. The band and the album just seemed to be a complete fit with my mind, beliefs, personality, life and ambitions: the songs told a tale of hobo travelling, nostalgia for better times and the search for more, partying excess, alienation from society, getting into trouble and paranoia.

The band seemed like the 1980s version of Jack Kerouac and the beats, who'd told of their trips across the states to California in the 1950s. They'd also been running from what they saw as humdrum existences they could not fit into, but what most people see as normality.

My mind had also failed to settle, and it just dreamt of escape while working at the mill where most other school drop-outs ended up. As with Kerouac and Axl Rose of Guns N' Roses, boredom and booze brought me trouble and delinquency, and my ambitions to travel the world became as much about mental escape as seeing the sights.

As well as being the memoir of a rock fan who was inspired to travel by Kerouac and those who followed him, this book is also the first account, as far as the author knows, of the 1980s worker-traveller communities in Europe and the Middle-East.

Thatcher's Britain was dystopian for those seeking freedom and fairness. The unions had been crippled and the Peace Convoy hippy travellers attacked and basically run out of the country. Europe and the Middle-East offered employment possibilities close to home, and many people preferred to cross the channel to live a freer nomadic life working and travelling with the seasons.

Life was anarchic and often messy in the worker traveller communities, as in the 1950s beat communes or 1980s LA rock clubs and parties. Level headed people wouldn't have been impressed, but we thrived on the highs and lows; laughs and tears. We fitted in on the outside.

Thanks to Chipmunka for publishing this book and providing a voice for people who always feel outside society, whatever country they live in. Many of the people in the worker-traveller communities seemed to have mental health issues, and if they hadn't been living rough around Europe they may have been homeless in the UK. Whether it was because of unhappy childhoods or adult alienation most had a reason for their situation, and their life stories were often fascinating. Chipmunka provides a platform for such people, and as Kerouac said, those who are mad for it are usually the most interesting. In this case it is the lost tribes of Thatcher's 1980s to a Guns N' Roses and rock music soundtrack. Cheers for the music guys, and all the other rock bands that made the 1980s a cool time to be young.

The Guns N' Roses Worker-Traveller

This is a factual memoir account.
Names have been changed to protect the privacy of the individuals involved.

Marc Latham

The Guns N' Roses Worker-Traveller

Chapter 1

The Kerouac Kid California Hitch: UK to Yugoslavia, via Belgium, France, Spain and Italy

Monday August 25th, 1987

I left the flat I'd grown up in on a clear sunny morning; I could have done with my mind having the same clarity, but I'd stayed up late listening to Guns n' Roses' *Appetite for Destruction*, which had just been released and was about to take the world by storm.

I'd planned to leave earlier, as I wanted to hitch across the UK from a small town in the wilds of south-west Wales to a port on the south-east of England that day. I was twenty-one, and planned to travel around Europe before heading to the United States; to emulate Kerouac's journey from east to west coast and finish off in Los Angeles, which was now home to my favourite Heavy Metal music.

The rucksack on my back was the only clue this was a different morning to usual, as I strolled into town taking in a landscape I thought was the entire world as a child, but instead of routinely turning left towards the centre I veered right, heading out to the edge of town. When I reached the first long straight I faced the outgoing traffic and stuck out my left thumb. It was the start of a pretty average hitching day, with short and long hitches and journeys, quiet and talkative drivers, and interesting and boring scenery; but it was also the first steps of a journey that would take me across all the populated continents.

After a few lifts with local people I reached the motorway after twenty miles, and then had a seventy mile lift with a lorry driver who turned out to be the father of my best primary school friend before they moved away. I crossed the Severn Bridge, where Bob Dylan once posed with *No Direction Home*, and travelled across England during the afternoon and evening; managing to by-pass London on the M25. At a service station thirty miles from Dover I met my first fellow traveller of the trip; he introduced himself as Tony from Bournemouth and said he'd been home for a week after a couple of years abroad. I was excited by the international hobo's reports of life on the road, and they whetted my appetite for the coming adventure. We were both heading to Dover so hitched together, and arrived after two lifts; the second was with a German chef who spoke with a Geordie accent, and he took us to the port even though it was out of his way. Another traveller approached us soon after we arrived and asked if we wanted to buy the return leg of his ticket to Ostend; Tony was heading to Calais so I bought the ticket and gave him half the financial saving. Then we exchanged addresses, wished each other luck and parted; it was the first of a travelling ritual I would become accustomed to over the following years. As the ferry departed I stayed out on deck until the white cliffs were out of sight, wondering when or if I would return, and then bedded down on the floor in my sleeping bag.

Europe beckoned when I awoke three hours later as the ferry docked. A woman enquired about my plans as I waited to disembark; she seemed concerned and wished me luck, and it felt good to be doing something seen by *normal* people as exciting and dangerous. I was leaving a world I saw as *comfortably numb*, and a society I'd rebelled against since before my teens; henceforth I could create my own world, and live by my own rules.

Customs wasn't a problem, and after changing money I hitched in motion towards the motorway; it wasn't long before I had my first lift on foreign soil, in a Belgian van. I'd only had two hours sleep during the night and was falling asleep in the front, so the driver suggested I moved to the back; I didn't need much arm-twisting and slept soundly until the lift ended on the edge of Brussels. It wasn't exactly a text-book debut for my new role as a dynamic international hitcher, but the extra kip was very welcome.

The first sign of a decline in my fortune was the rain that started to pour down as I reached the Paris exit and started hitching. I persevered for a while, but after my arm began to lock and my thumb wilt I returned to Brussels; I ate brunch on a step while willing the weather to improve! It didn't, but with my belly now full I reluctantly traipsed back to the exit and tried again. A wretched afternoon ended when a lorry pulled in; I'd almost given up hope, and didn't believe he'd stopped to give me a lift until I was in the cab! The lift took me beyond the deluge, but dropped me off on the motorway, so I hiked for an hour to the next pay toll. I had a lift from there with an old couple, although the man seemed unhappy I'd initially given Paris as my destination, before agreeing to Lille. It would have been difficult to communicate that I was just glad to get a lift, and anywhere heading out of Belgium was welcome.

I decided to call it a day, and erected my tent in a nearby field. However, as I completed the task to the best of my ability, which wasn't great, the rain returned with a vengeance; I jumped into the tent to escape another drenching, but found I was housed in a bog and the water followed me in! When the downpour relented I moved the tent to another part of the field, and although it was again a bit wonky and wouldn't have passed a safety inspection it was good enough to get a few hours shut-eye. In the morning I felt like packing up and returning home, and if it wasn't for the embarrassment I faced on my return, after going on about travelling for so long, I might have!

So the only way was forward, and despite the despondency of the morning I would reach Paris later that day. Firstly, three quick lifts took me to Lille, where I had a walk round, changed money at ten francs to the pound, and had bread, cheese and fruit for lunch; they were to become the staples of my hitching diet. I walked out to the Paris road, and another three lifts and five hours later I arrived on the edge of my destination; the last lift was from a mother and daughter in a small car, and the mother was driving at speeds the vehicle didn't look capable of most of the way. Deciding not to enter central Paris that night I intended sleeping in a car-park under a store until a man came down to lock up and politely asked me to leave. After a short walk I slept on the edge of a small road in my sleeping bag, with my rucksack for a pillow, and my Swiss-army knife open in my hand. However, it was quite exposed there, and I awoke cold in the early morning, so I returned to the underground car park and slept outside the entrance, as it was at least sheltered from the wind.

I got a few hours kip, and in the morning took the metro to the Champs-Elysées, before walking up the Champ de Mars, becoming increasingly excited as I neared the Eiffel Tower. I paid the twenty-two francs entrance fee, and after walking up the first two levels was relieved there was an escalator for the third, as I was carrying a rucksack that included everything bar the kitchen sink! It was worth it though, as there was a superb view from the top. My spirits were lifted after the calamities of the previous day, and I was starting to think I'd made the right decision; I was in Paris, the sun was shining and the sky was blue. I wasn't to know it at the time, but the good weather was to last for the rest of the hitch. After a few hours in and around the Eiffel Tower I visited the Place Georges Pompidou, where a mix of skateboarders and roller-skaters, music, and vendors selling various wares made it a colourful and entertaining place to spend an afternoon and evening. However, I also thought of the lads at home starting the usual weekend of excess, and half wished I was back there, *in a bar where everyone knows your name*.

I planned to sleep under the Eiffel Tower so I returned there as it got dark, but I noticed there was a man following me after arriving, so I legged it. After losing him I slept behind a wall on the banks of the Seine. I woke happy, as the morning was again bathed in glorious sunshine. I celebrated by washing my hair and upper body in a fountain, and changed a shirt! After a bread and cheese breakfast I walked through some nice gardens and Le Concorde to the Louvre. As I sat outside on a wall some motorbikes went whizzing past with people filming or taking photos on the back, and when I looked over the wall Madonna was running on the banks of the Seine with bodyguards in tow. That night she would play to 130,000 people at Parc de Sceaux in Paris; a record attendance for a concert in France at the time.

After the entourage disappeared as quickly as it had arrived I walked to the Notre Dame, where I relaxed reading and writing. At the time I had a *Kerrang* magazine, and *Hitch-hiker's Guide to Europe* and *Easy*

Riders books, and during the journey I wrote a diary, letters and postcards. At the end of the day I returned to the Louvre, as I'd seen a good sleeping place inside a gate by the entrance, and it also offered the novelty of sleeping at a world famous site. However, after opening the knife it cut my finger, causing it to bleed quite heavily until I wrapped it with some cloth that came with the tent. Another couple of travellers later came inside to sleep; I wonder if they still think about the night they slept at the Louvre?

I tried to enter the gallery in the morning, but the staff told me rucksacks weren't allowed and advised me to store it at the train station. So I left intending to return, but after reaching the station found the lockers were only available for forty-eight hour time slots; I'd planned on leaving the next day, and because I felt so pissed-off I hadn't stored my rucksack earlier I decided to leave Paris and *head out on the highway*. Therefore, I took a train out to Massey-Palaiseau; the final station on the south-west Paris line.

After reaching M-P and ascending into daylight I thought the scenery looked like something out of a Spaghetti Western, with the sun spreading its rays over an arid environment and any human activity moving in Sunday morning slow motion. I found the motorway, but there was a hitcher already there, so I started walking, hoping to find a smaller road joining the motorway or a pay-toll. However, after a few miles there was nothing in sight, so I just sat down and hitched; it felt surreal, and became even more so ten minutes later when a driver stopped and provided a 150 mile lift to Angers. The businessman spoke some English and bought me a beer at a café on the way, which made it even better. After a tough morning it was the kind of lift I'd really needed, and life on the road didn't seem as bad anymore; after entering the Loire valley the scenery also became more interesting, and we passed the Le Mans racetrack. However, my exhilaration was tempered slightly after the lift ended when I realised it would probably have been advantageous to stay in the car until Nantes, as it was further south than Angers.

Feeling the serotonin dissipate I trudged over to a small green enclave between roads and had a snooze between unsuccessful attempts to hitch. I ended up staying there the night and had a good sleep apart from occasionally sliding down the slight slope! The next day I had a lift to Nantes with a Frenchman who didn't speak much English, but was interested in making conversation; he wanted me to speak French, and I remembered a few words from school. I bought some food and water in Nantes before heading out on the Poitiers road.

As I left town a car stopped ahead of me and a man said he was heading to Poitiers. I put my rucksack in the car-boot on his invitation and sat in the front seat. He had a photo of a woman and two children on the dashboard, but started to worry me when he stroked my arm while asking about my tattoos, and then my bare leg. So I asked if the woman in the photo was his wife and he said no, he was gay. This freaked me out due to the circumstances of him picking me up and having the photo on his dashboard, and I demanded he let me out at the next roundabout. He complied.

I saw I was near a village called Vallet, which was renowned for its wine, and as wine-picking in the region was one of the jobs recommended in the *Hitchhiker's Guide* I thought I'd have a look. However, the shops were shut and there was silence all around, so I was quite relieved when an old woman I asked about work said there wasn't any. I headed out of the village, but didn't have any liquid and wasn't confident of getting a lift, with the motorway eight miles away. I was therefore mightily relieved when a lorry driver gave me a lift to the edge of Nantes, even though it was a backward step for my journey!

The silver lining on the metaphorically cloudy day started shining vociferously ten minutes later when I had a hundred mile lift with an electronics worker to Rochefort; he was from Brittany and said he was returning to work for the week. We drove through picturesque villages parallel with the west coast, and had a good conversation about national service, Celts, football, music, and his trips to Ireland and London. After he dropped me off I had a lift to Bordeaux half an hour later, so despite a few hiccups along the way I'd covered 200 miles in two lifts, and was in love with hitch-hiking again!

I walked round town after eating, and ended up reading and writing in a park near a street with trendy shops, cafés and people. I felt good about the day but also quite lonely, and a tad jealous of the locals on their normal night out: meeting friends, eating and drinking, and going home to a bed. I tried sleeping on a park bench, but a couple arguing nearby prevented me settling there, and I ended up behind a wall in the grounds of the castle. I brushed my teeth using limeade instead of water in the morning, before setting off for the motorway. After reaching the edge of the road I could see rain approaching, with the distant hills being turned from green to grey by the misty cloud of precipitation. I prepared myself for a soaking, but just as the first spots of liquid reached me a car pulled up and took me beyond the storm. My luck continued through the morning, and another couple of lifts took me to the

The Guns N' Roses Worker-Traveller

Spanish border.

My final lift of the day was with three German students, and they were heading to San Sebastian: my destination for the day. The scenery changed dramatically as we entered the Pyrenees, with picturesque red-roofed white houses speckled around the lush green mountains. One of the students spoke good English, and after I enthused about the German rock band, the Scorpions, he put their *Worldwide Live* tape on the stereo, which made my day. They also gave me some food along the way, and bought me a coffee in San Sebastian after we arrived. After a stroll around town and the beach we said goodbye and they continued on their journey towards the west coast.

I sat on the Playa de la Concha sea-front, under the constant glare of the Christ statue on Monte Urgull; it made San Sebastian resemble a mini Rio de Janeiro for me. While there, I declined an offer of hash from two blokes from Reading, because I didn't want any rather than for fear of offending Jesus, but talked to them for a while. They recommended the train station as a good place to sleep, but it didn't look safe when I later checked it out, mostly because some urchins had filled an old mattress with bottles before setting it alight, and the glass was exploding as I arrived! So I walked for a while, before sleeping behind some bushes at an entrance to a building.

After I'd entered deep sleep another traveller woke me without realising, and in return I startled him as I stirred. After recovering his composure he asked if he could use the other side of my rucksack as a pillow. I agreed before returning to the land of nod. Just after waking in the morning a local approached with a red face looking like steam would soon come surging out of his ears, so we made our excuses as best we could and left. We finally got around to introducing ourselves once we were clear, and my fellow traveller introduced himself as Mahar from Glasgow; he was heading home on a Euro-rail ticket. After brekkie we spent the day on the playa, with the sol shining strong enough to sunbathe. At the end of the day I had a shower on the beach, and cleansed myself of most of the grubbiness a body attracts during nine days tramping! After scran and plonk in a park we frequented a few bars: the first had a Heavy Metal theme, and there were some Metallers inside; I couldn't communicate with them verbally, but showed them my *Monsters of Rock* t-shirt and *Kerrang* to let them know I was one of them. It was a good night, and I was half sloshed when we finished drinking at midnight. Mahar got the train to Paris an hour later, after warning me to watch myself, as he didn't think I was streetwise enough to survive the trip; I assured him I was. It had been a brief but good encounter, as most were *on the road*. I returned to the previous night's resting place and crashed out.

      I felt hot and hung-over in the morning, and matters weren't helped by initially hiking in the wrong direction, so I sat down for a while resting and psyching, before walking back into San Sebastian to find the correct road. After eventually getting my first hitch of the day I was dropped off in front of a timber-mill on the edge of a small town. It reminded me of my only full-time job, as I'd worked in a similar place after leaving school; it had been where most of the men in town with no direction started working, and the pay had financed my journey. While the work was mostly monotonous, and winter days often freezing in the open shed, there was a good community spirit, and the holiday breaking-up parties were legendary.

The Guns N' Roses Worker-Traveller

The next lift took me to Pamplona, and as it was getting late I walked to the southern edge of town, set my sleeping-bag out behind a wall and slept. I'd decided to thumb for Barcelona the next day and then return to France, as hitching was too difficult in Spain; I wondered if it was my tattoos, as I'd noticed there weren't many in Spain, and felt people were staring at me more than in France.

My troubles continued in the morning, as it took me hours to get a lift, but when it eventually came it proved to be worth the wait. It was with a couple of dudes that reminded me of the characters in the *Cheech and Chong* films, and they even shared a joint with me as we travelled through the desert to a Spanish folk-music soundtrack. After they dropped me off in Tudela I switched from a sixties hippy mind-set to the nineteenth century Wild-West. Initially it was because the town's name reminded me of Toledo in the US, but it was mainly because of the parched white-washed houses landscape. Most Spaghetti Westerns were made in Spain, and as I walked through dry and dusty streets I imagined I was *The Man With No Name*; an outlaw passing through a town of law-abiding Hispanic people.

From Tudela I had a cool lift with a bloke who put AC/DC's *Let There Be Rock* tape on and gave me water; the liquid intake was invaluable, as I'd run out, and would soon become stranded for the afternoon. The next lift took me forty miles but ended on the north-western edge of Zaragoza, with the Los Monegros desert surrounding me, no decent hitching spot in sight, and the sun still *red hot*.

I started walking, but another hitcher soon caught up with me, and we introduced ourselves as Argentinean and British. These disclosures brought a short silence, as the Falklands War was still a vivid memory. Who knows, maybe he fought there!? He was alright though, and at the time we were just two people united by extreme circumstances. He said he was heading to a petrol station fifteen miles ahead and eventually faded into the distant heat.

I continued walking, and was passed by an army convoy; when I saw soldiers looking out from the back of the trucks I wondered if they wanted my freedom, pitied my situation, or were just indifferent. I didn't know how they felt, but I envied their purpose in life a little, their companionship a bit more, and their transport and motion immensely! I continued hitching in motion for a few hours, from one side of Zaragoza to the other, with no water, my shoulders and upper spine aching, and the back of the rucksack soaked with sweat filtered through my shirt. At the time I bitterly regretted venturing into Spain, but later became thankful for the experience and memories.

The hardship also made the next lift all the sweeter. I was about to stop for the night and sleep on the edge of the highway when a car pulled up ahead. I didn't think they'd stopped for me at first, but when I reached the car a friendly Spanish couple welcomed me. The relief was indescribable as I made myself comfortable in the rear, and I felt overwhelming gratitude towards them. I said I was going to Barcelona but I don't think they heard or understood me, as the city came and went on our right; I didn't protest, and wasn't that sorry, as I half wanted the lift to continue as long as possible. In the end it was worth it, as they continued driving for a further hour or two. It was close to midnight when they dropped me off near to the French border in the small town of Figueres, so I didn't look around for long before sleeping on a line of grass separating two

The Guns N' Roses Worker-Traveller

roads. It wasn't ideal, and there were slugs on my sleeping-bag in the morning!

Salvador Dali was born in Figueres, and I hiked up a steep hill to a museum dedicated to him in the morning, but found it was closed when I arrived; however, there was one of his sculptures outside, so I tried to convince myself the walk had been worthwhile. After returning to the centre of town another traveller sat near me, and after we started talking it turned out he lived forty miles away from me. As the afternoon morphed into evening we bought a bottle of plonk each and drank them at the bench, until a downpour forced us under a nearby balcony. After draining the wine we frequented a bar and bought a round of beer each; it had a video jukebox on, and Whitesnake, Waysted and Gary Moore played. We stayed until closing and slept in a backyard in town. After waking the next morning we waited for the toilets to open, but being a Sunday they didn't, so we had a coffee in a café and used the toilets there. Ready for the day, we traipsed to the edge of town, undertook the goodbye ritual, and headed in opposite directions; it had been another nice interlude in the lonesome hitching marathon. I walked a couple of miles, and used the rest of my pesetas on a burger and ice-cream along the way. After starting to hitch I soon had a lift to the border with a bloke from Luxembourg who spoke good English and played Deep Purple all the way.

We crossed the border without a passport check, and he dropped me off at Le Perthus soon afterwards. I started hitching after walking to a suitable place, and a car with GB plates going in the other direction pulled up. We started talking and they said they were RAF personnel stationed in Germany on their way to windsurf in Lloret de Mar; they were waiting for another car and gave me a couple of beers before their friends arrived and they continued south. I was again filled with doubts about whether I was doing this travelling lark the right way, but told myself you couldn't expect non-stop highs on a *permanent vacation*.

It was quite a while before I had my next lift, and it was a bit of a strange one when it arrived: a big car stopped and the driver asked for petrol money if I wanted a lift north; I replied I was heading south-east and didn't want to pay, and he said I could have a lift to Perpignan for nothing. I accepted and entered, joining five people in three rows of seats. They said they were travelling up from Morocco, so I thought spending time on the Mediterranean gave us something special in common, but when I mentioned heading to Greece for the winter they weren't impressed, and said it wasn't the same.

After reaching the edge of Perpignan I gave myself an hour more hitching time as it was getting dark. Less than half that time had elapsed when I got an excellent short lift in a Triumph-convertible, with warm coastal wind blowing the day's physical and mental detritus away within ten miles. I felt refreshed and on a roll, so although it was quite dark I started hitching again; lo and behold it wasn't long before I had another lift in a nice car to the edge of Narbonne, whereupon I contentedly called it a day.

I met a Finnish couple looking for somewhere to change money in town the next morning; they were in an upbeat mood because it was another beautiful day and they'd heard it was near freezing in Helsinki! After starting to hitch I had a good day, with a few lifts taking me to the French Riviera; the last was with a Milanese called David, who'd travelled quite extensively himself.

The Guns N' Roses Worker-Traveller

It was a long lift, and after seeing the sun set over a beautiful cove along the way we ended up in Cassis, near Marseille. David bought me a beer and sandwich before going to meet his French girlfriend. After he left I relaxed on the beach, and in the evening walked through town to look for water and somewhere to sleep; I found a tap and slept at the side of some flats. I carried on recuperating by the sea the next day, and the only downer was a local shouting at me for washing my hair in a fountain!

As I was about to use my stove for the first time in the evening another traveller asked if I knew anywhere to sleep. After I told him about the previous night's experience and we introduced ourselves Uwe bought some beers and we shared them and the food I cooked. He was from a coal-mining town in the north of Germany and was also hitching to Rome. At the end of the night we bedded down in our sleeping bags on the beach, but I didn't sleep well; probably because we were out in the open and right in front of the village. Uwe went to a café for brekkie in the morning while I looked for stamps; a middle-aged local showed me to the post office in the end! I rejoined Uwe, and after a coffee we took turns hitching. We got a lift each, and one was with a German; Uwe sat in front talking to him, but later said he didn't understand much as the driver was from the south. He dropped us off on the other side of Toulon, where we got stuck, although we were offered two lifts neither wanted to take both of us. We admitted defeat in the end and decided to split; before parting we went one better than the standard goodbye ritual by arranging to meet outside St. Peter's church the following Tuesday at 6 p.m. if we'd reached Rome. Uwe caught a bus to Hijeres, while I continued hitching without any luck.

Marc Latham

I needed a break and sat down to cook a tin of potatoes, carrots and peas; as the food boiled a *pretty woman* made my day when she wished me *bon appétit* in that cute French accent. After the food I started hitching in motion, and my perseverance was rewarded with a lift from three girls; the sudden female attention made me wonder if my pheromones had launched a mass breakout! A lift to Carqueiranne followed, and after the day's trials and tribulations the evening was again making up for it; I felt in a wonderful mood and on another roll. This developed into a hitching euphoria after a further two lifts, and I would have married hitching that night if it had a physical form; the second lift came after I had all but finished for the day, and half-heartedly stuck my thumb out. After getting dropped off in a beach resort called St. Maxime I bedded down between the back of a caravan and a wall. I slept okay, but in the morning some people in the caravan awoke at the same time as me, so I quickly packed and scarpered.

I had a few lifts in the morning, including one with a local who said he studied English at Nice University and liked *Bauhaus* and *Lords of the New Church* music, until reaching a spot with another hitcher already there. We got talking, and he introduced himself as Pieter from Australia. We were both heading to Nice so we hitched together, and soon got a lift to our mutual destination. Pieter sat in the front during the lift, and I heard him tell the driver he was South African; I brought this up afterwards, and he explained that he rarely admitted his nationality in Europe, as it often provoked a bad reaction because of the Apartheid system. He said he knew of a cheap hotel in Nice so I agreed to share, as a proper bed sounded good and I could wash some clothes. We walked around the city in the evening, and the centre was bustling with a colourful mix of buskers, street artists, locals and tourists. I watched music videos on television after returning to the hotel, before sleeping like the proverbial log.

Pieter was staying in Nice for three nights, so I bade him farewell the next day without much ritual and set off. It took ages to hike up a long road out of the city, but on the positive side there was a fantastic view; Nice lived up to its name! After reaching the brow of the hill I had a short lift to a small village sitting atop high cliffs that dropped steeply down to white sand and blue-green sea coves. I walked through the hamlet and out *on the road*; for once, I wasn't bothered about hiking in heat with a heavy rucksack, as I was enjoying the view so much. After reaching another village the vista euphoria swirling through my mind made me buy a bottle of wine with my last francs; well, that's my excuse anyway!

At the end of that village I stopped and hitched, and soon had a lift to Monaco; my destination for the day. After getting dropped off I made my way over to Monte Carlo Avenue for a nice view over the harbour, before cooking some beans to eat with my wine. Smartly dressed people passed on their way to the casino or some other event, and it was entertaining watching their reactions as they passed a raggedy arsed wino cooking chow. When in Monaco don't do as the locals do!

A group of young people also passed, and I laughed when one shouted *what's for tea?* Three of them later returned and introduced themselves as Antipodeans on a bus trip round Europe; they also invited me to a bar called Rosie's, but I said I didn't have any francs left. However, after they left I realised I still had £1.25 in coins, so after finishing my grub and grog I joined them at Rosie's. They greeted me warmly when I entered, and after changing my coins with one of them for ten francs I bought a beer. After an initial conversation about the pros and cons of our respective travels; they envied my freedom of time and place, and I was jealous of their comfort and companionship; I started talking to an attractive New Zealander called Sarah more than the originals, which I felt guilty about after we'd said our goodbyes and they'd caught their bus to Rome. I went over to the casino and stood amongst the crowd watching the well-attired arriving and departing, before sleeping in the dingy corner of a multi-story car park.

After resuming my hike in the morning I saw Monaco were playing Bordeaux in a football match later and thought about watching it, but continued walking to the eastern edge of town at the same time. As I studied my European road-map while sitting on the street a bus luckily stopped in front of me, as it brought the cars behind to a standstill, and the driver of one asked where I was going. When I told him Genoa he waved me in and drove me there; sometimes hitching is truly heavenly! He was a chef in the south of France and at the end of the lift gave me his address and told me he'd *gimme shelter* if I returned; he was visiting another man in Genoa so I thought he was probably gay, but he never tried it on or anything and was cool.

I'd reached Italy, home of many culinary delights, but I lunched on bread, cheese and water before walking into town. Once in the centre I asked a local where I could change money, but was told the train station was the only place open on a Saturday, and it was in the opposite direction! So I walked back to it, having nice eye contact with a beautiful woman on the way, and changed a £20 traveller's cheque at about

The Guns N' Roses Worker-Traveller

2,000 lire to the pound. I had another two lifts after that, but only between pay tolls on the edge of Genoa, and a few laughs with other drivers giving *short lift* or *other direction* gestures; *all the world's a stage*! After calling it a day I saw there was some five-a-side football being played in a floodlit complex, so I went over and watched it from outside the fence and bedded down there after they'd finished. I slept well, and as the next morning was a Sunday I took it easy at first, writing some diary and watching more football.

After starting to hitch I had another lift to the original pay toll, before a couple with a young baby gave me a fifty mile lift to near Sarzana; they only spoke a little English but communicated that their boy was twenty months old, and the man had liked Britain when he'd visited. After they dropped me off I hitched behind a toll for ages, until another hobo started hitching towards Genoa from in front of it, and had a lift after ten minutes. I thought it was a bit cheeky, but decided to try from in front myself, and soon had a lift with a couple. Had I been doing it wrong until then!? The couple who picked me up didn't speak much English, but we made some conversation and they put the Pisa v AC Milan game on the radio, although it was in Italian so I couldn't understand much! At the end of the lift they went out of their way to leave me in a good spot on the edge of Pisa.

I could see the leaning tower as soon as they dropped me off, and *walked that way*. It was an interesting sight that I'd known about since childhood, so I was glad I'd resisted the opportunity to continue south with my lift. After having a look round I was sitting on the grass when two tourists asked if I'd take a photo of them. I duly obliged, and one also took a photo of me with the other. They took my address and said they'd send a copy, but it never arrived; the *photo-sending broken promise* was another norm I became accustomed to *on the road*.

I left the square after a few hours and treated myself to a Pizza Marguerita outside a café; it was my first food of the day, and I rewarded my thoroughly awakened taste buds for their patience with a delicious tub of strawberry and raspberry ice cream. Then I came across a tap in the street and washed my hair, before seeing the AC Milan president with a crowd of people getting his autograph. I thought we were most definitely on different ends of the social scale: the president and the pauper! I headed out from the centre in the evening, stopping along the way to watch a football match and mini-carnival. Upon arrival at the Rome road I found myself on an open building site, as another lane was being added, and bedded down amidst it for a sound sleep.

Two lifts got me to the Florence turn-off in the morning; the second was from a Pisa fan who said they'd lost 3-1 to Milan. He also got me a lift to the centre after dropping me off. I hadn't originally planned on visiting Florence, but had been advised it would be quicker travelling south that way and it was a beautiful city. After reaching the centre I bought a *giant peach*, a massive apple and some nuts; the man on the stall didn't like it when I handled the fruit to check them. I went over to the main square to eat, before strolling around the impressive buildings that encircled it, and the quaint Ponte Vecchio Bridge. I watched the buskers and artists during the evening, before bedding down by the side of a house, hidden from the street by a railings foundation; the gate to the garden had been open. After a decent sleep I was about to leave when I heard voices; I looked round the corner of the house and saw

The Guns N' Roses Worker-Traveller

a man guiding a car out, before locking the gate and entering the house. I rushed to the front but that exit was also shackled. So I threw my rucksack over the fence ready to follow it stealthily, only for my glass water bottle to fall out and smash on the floor. Panic induced adrenalin surged through my body, and after quickly climbing over the fence I collected my rucksack before breaking into a fast walk past some startled pedestrians!

My troubles continued after reaching the highway, as I had no luck hitching. I think I was saved by the last remnants of adrenalin, as something inspired me to scribble *per favore* on my Roma sign; the magic words did the trick, and a good lift soon followed. I was confident it wouldn't be long before my next lift after I received friendly gestures from several drivers, and sure enough I soon had a lift straight to Rome. It was off a scrap-dealer driving a truck towing a smashed car. He said his name was Dino, he was thirty, and his wife was expecting their first baby. The truck kept cutting out, and I helped him siphon petrol from one side to the other, getting my hands greasy in the process. He'd been working for twelve hours but was still driving like a *bat out of hell* as we entered Rome, swerving between heavy traffic in our path. Dino advised me to take a bus after dropping me off on the edge of Rome, but I hiked for an hour towards the centre before realising it was too far to walk! I read and wrote the evening away while sitting against a wall, before sleeping behind some flats.

I frequented a nearby convenience store in the morning, but an old man chucked me out *talking Italian*, with his demeanour leaving me in no doubt what he meant. I don't know why he was hostile, but guessed he was either aware of me sleeping rough nearby or just didn't like my appearance: *barbarian at the gates of Rome syndrome*? I laughed at him and scarpered, catching the bus to the centre after buying two 700 lire tickets at the bus stop; I later regretted my acquisition after nobody asked for them on the bus or when I transferred to a tram. I'd arrived in Rome, but too late to meet Uwe.

However, I was to get some much needed company after all, because while I was at the train-station looking for information a Canadian called Chuck persuaded me to stay at the campsite he was working for; it was only 7500 lire a night and I'd thought about getting accommodation anyway, as I needed a rest and wash. He said you could buy a bus ticket that lasted from 2 p.m.-midnight for 1,000 lire, so we got one each and travelled to the campsite together; we had to change buses in Sempione, and he bought me a slice of pizza as we waited for the connection. Chuck said he'd been in Europe for three years.

They took my passport when I checked in, as you paid at the end of your stay, before showing me to the accommodation shed; it consisted of four double bunks on each side of a walkway, and reminded me of the convict quarters in *Cool Hand Luke*. There were two lads in mine, and they introduced themselves as Ross and Chris: Ross was from Canada and had been cycling round Europe for six months, while Chris was British and had been in Europe for two years busking with his banjo.

After introductions we relocated to some tables just below the cabins, where lime green leaves shaded us from golden sunshine falling from a clear blue sky. The idyllic setting set the mood for the day, and everybody just chilled at the tables or in the two hammocks strung between sturdy branches, boozing and smoking while playing games

The Guns N' Roses Worker-Traveller

and talking about the usual stuff. We also tried cooking adjacent to the tables, but ended up with cold vegetables and burnt pasta; I didn't let it go to waste however, and ate quite a lot! Apart from Ross and Chris I mostly talked with Tommy, a Scot who collected money for Chris while he busked; an Englishwoman called Kate who used to live thirty miles away from me and knew an old friend who'd joined a rock band called Atom Seed; and an Irishman named Tynan, who was returning overland after holidaying in Corfu. We called Tynan *Conan*, after the barbarian; although his name was similar his thin frame and placid nature meant he was the opposite in every other way. I talked to Ross quite a lot about Heavy Metal, as he'd been to several concerts and knew about the LA scene I was most interested in. Chris crashed out soon after sunset, and Tommy and I later carried him to the cabin before calling it a day. I'd thoroughly enjoyed the day, and it was nice to be amongst humanity again, having conversations and a laugh with like-minded people. I'd yearned for company before Rome, and thought myself fortunate to have found such a nice crowd.

I felt rough in the morning, but also happy and content, as I could hear the others talking and felt at home. My head felt better after a shower, and I joined the others in humorous conversation on another beautiful day. Ross later agreed to go sightseeing in Rome with me, even though he'd been before, and we travelled to the centre *on the buses* in the afternoon; we didn't bother buying tickets, as checks were apparently rare. We had a good walk and got to most of the main attractions, with the Coliseum and St. Peter's Basilica the highlights. We finished off at the Trevi fountain, and got pizza and ice-cream in Sempione on the way back. After returning to the camp we joined the others for a good evening's chatter; nobody drank much but the conversation still flowed until late. I bussed into the centre with Tynan the next day, while Ross rode in. After liaising at the train station I gooned round on Ross's bike like Butch in *Butch Cassidy and the Sundance Kid*. After a carefree stroll in the sun we met Chris and Tommy at the Spanish Steps before returning to the camp together.

It was Chuck's birthday the next day, and after lazing in the sun through the morning a few of us ventured down to Sempione to buy food and alcohol for the party in the afternoon. We were in a great mood already, and after meeting others from the camp in the shop we returned on a real high. Tynan and Ross cooked the food on my stove, and it went perfectly this time. The manager of the campsite also brought a cake out for Eddie, and we all had a piece. I boozed all night, and had a great time as far as I could remember, but the next day got told that I later fell asleep at the table and was sick over myself. We continued partying in the morning, which was again gloriously sunny, finishing off the food, smoke and alcohol during another classic day.

We had a great laugh talking about the weekend on Monday morning, and the chuckles just kept coming. Firstly, the cleaner started spraying us with the hose, and we all moved out of the way apart from Tynan, who was too hung-over to move; and then Ross spent ages washing his sweatshirt and hung it on the clothes-line, only for a cat to knock it into the dirt soon after. Ross, Tynan and I were supposed to leave that day, so we all checked out and went down to the city. We also met Tommy and Chris there to say goodbye, but as it turned out, none of us left: I thought it was too late to start hitching, Tynan still felt unwell and Ross just couldn't be bothered. Despite lethargy and sobriety we had another entertaining night, with everybody reminiscing about our time together. We also picked out each other's funny characteristics, with my accent and habit of drunkenly falling asleep on the table the main ones attributed to me. After going to bed I couldn't sleep for ages, as I felt hot and wired; it could have been my subconscious trying to rebel against my sleepy image, but was more likely to have been the dry-horrors!

I rose at 8 a.m., having earlier heard Tommy and Chris leave to go busking. I washed and went through the leaving ritual with Ross and Tynan, and also arranged to meet Ross in an Athens hostel if we were there at the same time; it didn't happen, but we met again on my third journey six years later. I was sad to be leaving a place and time I'd loved, and people I'd bonded with, to go back on the road alone, but that is the nature of independent travelling my friend; and as the old adage goes, you've got to take the rough with the smooth.

I started hitching northwards to Venice from outside the campsite and soon had a lift to Orte, where I decided to travel via a different route to the journey south. So I swapped roads to ramble east across the Apennines, and had two quick lifts through glorious mountain scenery. I was dropped off in a secluded spot, and feeling like a *desolation angel* back *on the road* amidst almost unspoilt nature I had time to ponder, reflecting on my time in Rome and how quickly the friendships had formed and ended; a few hours after leaving my first community away from home the hole in the shack gang was now just memories, and that time had gone.

I walked awhile, before having a lift with a female journalist who edited eight pages on a Rimini newspaper. She bought me a coffee along the way and we talked politics, as she was in the Communist party. I then had another three lifts before realising one of the eggs in my rucksack had broken, leaving my clothes inside stinking; another had cracked and I ate it raw. I continued thumbing, but my successful hitching day went pear-shaped after that; or should that be egg-shaped?! I got another lift, but following a bungled drop-off the next driver that stopped informed me I was hitching the wrong way for Venice!

It was already quite dark, but I walked back down the motorway, scrambled up a grass bank and climbed over a barbed wire fence separating different sections of the road. It was 9.30 p.m. by the time I settled down amongst some bushes on the side of the road, and I hadn't eaten all day. So I sat under a light and ate pasta, tomatoes and the eggs I had left, before updating the diary. I got into the sleeping bag just after midnight, and noticed the grass was wet from a heavy mist that had descended.

I didn't sleep well, and after waking saw a thick fog had cut visibility to twenty feet. There didn't seem much chance of getting a lift where I was, so I started walking; I knew it was quite dangerous under the conditions but I didn't think I had much option. After walking for half an hour I saw a sign stating Padova was still six miles away, and felt drained and dejected. However, a silver lining in the fog soon appeared; I was picked up and taken to a toll about three miles away, and ten minutes later got a lift with a lorry driver to the edge of Venice. The journey took ages because traffic was usually travelling at a snail's pace or stationary, with regular vehicle pile-ups on either side of the motorway testament to the density of the fog.

After getting dropped off I took a local bus into

The Guns N' Roses Worker-Traveller

Venice without paying. I walked round the canals at first finding my bearings, and despite the murky weather washed my hair under a convenient tap. Then I found the train station and got a map of Venice after storing my rucksack. I hiked more during the afternoon and evening, visiting the Piazza San Marco and the port; seeing big cargo ships surprised me, as I'd imagined Venice to be just a small picturesque city containing nothing more than canals and tourists. At the end of the day I climbed over a fence into an apartment complex with trees and gardens around the edge, and bedded down amid the vegetation. In the morning I jumped back over the fence and heard a shout as I left, but just kept walking. I bought food and shampoo with the last of my small lire and took a bus out to the motorway; it looked very different under a clear sky.

I hitched in motion before having a lift to the Portogruaro exit, where a policeman moved me from behind a toll to before it. It was the first time the police had interfered with my hitching on the trip, and they ended up doing me a favour, as I had a lift soon after. Thinking back to Genoa, an Italian-looking gentleman had hitched from before the toll, so I deduced you were deemed to be on the motorway after the toll, and therefore supposed to hitch from in front! I just thought it was more polite to request lifts from drivers when they were in motion rather than stationary; when like a trapped target they had little chance of escaping your pleading gaze!

The lift was off a bloke without much spare space in his car, and I shared the back seat with a mountain bike! I then had another two lifts, but the second dropped me off on the motorway. I started walking but saw some police ahead in the distance, and thought I'd better avoid them, so I walked up the grass bank and climbed over a wall at the top. I dropped onto a farm track, where a surprised farmer watched me pass without comment; his dogs barked for a while. I could see four policemen stopping vehicles below, so I crept along the top of the embankment until they were out of sight, and then returned to the motorway.

An hour later I was relieved to receive a lift to Trieste off an old bloke who said he worked for the British Transport Battalion as a prisoner of war during World War Two; his young companion moved into the back so I could sit in the front. I ate some food in Trieste and walked out hitching, but the traffic sped past without time for my sorry arse, making me regret not catching a local bus as far as possible. After two frustrating hours I stopped for food on the side of the road, and ended up staying there the night, initially bedding down near a tennis-court where people were still playing. I was knackered and nodded off quickly, but a thunderstorm later woke me. I tried to see it out where I was but in the end ran across the road to a bus shelter and bedded down there, after changing my t-shirt for a jumper; the sleeping-bag was wet on the outside, but dry inside. The shelter was outside what looked like an important building and in full view of the road, but I soon fell into a deep sleep. I'd heard it was near impossible to get lifts in Yugoslavia and was thinking about getting public transport there, as I was sick of hitching!

Chapter 2

From Hitching Hell to Purgatory: Yugoslavia, mainland Greece and early Crete

After rising early and hitching in motion towards Yugoslavia I had a lift to the border with a postie; it was my eighty-sixth lift. Going through customs I was thrilled to receive my first passport stamp of the journey, and after changing £20 at about 1400 dinars to the pound bought some food. It cost next to nothing, and this was literally true, as I'd just found a 1,000 dinar note on the floor: *dirty deeds done dirt cheap*!

I tried hitching from the border, but what little traffic there was consisted mostly of small cars full of people. This confirmed everything I'd heard or read about it. Those people that noticed the scruffy traveller just looked at me incredulously, and in the end I started walking toward a nearby town all but having decided to pay for transport through Yugoslavia. I still tried hitching as I walked, but then came across a bus-stop and saw there was a bus to Ljubljana due. So I stopped there, flagged the bus down and left not only the hitching behind for a few days, but also my attempt to thumb all the way to Athens.

As I made myself comfortable with two seats to myself I felt a mixture of relief and disappointment; but I thought I'd made the correct decision after we ascended into the mountains on a small road with little traffic. There was also great scenery, with orange- roofed white houses dotted around verdant hills that overlooked a tranquil deep blue sea. Moreover, it was only 2,000 dinars for the eighty mile journey.

I received some quizzical looks after arriving in Ljubljana, and wasn't sure if it was my tattoos, shorts, or overall scruffy appearance. The counter-staff at the train-station weren't very helpful, but I managed to buy a ticket to Belgrade for 4,000 dinars. The train left an hour later, and I spent most of the intervening time having a long #2 in an impressive toilet.

It was crowded on the train but I eventually found a compartment with a spare seat. Apart from me it contained two soldiers, a couple, and three single men; one of whom was Greek. As I settled into the journey several policemen turned up to check passports, and then started demanding money. I complained when they asked me, but the man in the couple told me I had to give 1,000 dinars, so I handed it over begrudgingly. I tried to watch the view as much as possible, but it got dark an hour after passing through Zagreb, so I started reading *Easy Riders*. One of the soldiers asked to see it, and smiled at the cover-picture of a biker on a chopper with a woman in stockings riding pillion. Later, a mother and daughter of about forty and twenty years of age came into the compartment; the daughter could speak English and we talked about politics, Yugoslavia, travelling, work and tattoos. A bloke sitting the other side of me tried to enter the conversation and asked me to read his Serbo-Croat identity card out; I went along with that, but refused when he asked me to read a full page of small print. Then he elaborately played around with his calculator, but I ignored him, and continued talking to the daughter, who gave me a blackcurrant sweet. After the lights went off everybody seemed to sleep; except me. Rain fell heavily outside, which again made me relieved to not be hitching, although I half suspected I was still trying to convince myself the right decision had been made.

The Guns N' Roses Worker-Traveller

We arrived in Belgrade an hour before midnight, twenty minutes late. The overcrowding made disembarking difficult, although I wasn't exactly in a rush, as only darkness and drizzle awaited. After my piss briefly brightened the dank station toilet I hastily exited the squalid building. Three mangy cats eyed me closely as I entered the *big city night*, and their interest intensified after I started tucking into some bread and cheese I still had from the border; my arrival in Yugoslavia that morning seemed a long time ago now! The cats and I were soon moved on by a street-cleaning team, and I started searching for somewhere to sleep. I chose a block of flats where the bottom floor was sheltered and dry, but had to wait for a man exercising on the balcony to go inside first. I slept okay, but one of the doors opened early in the morning, and a bloke came out to investigate. He was followed by a couple from the next flat. I motioned my apologies, packed and shuffled away.

I read the *Hitch-hiker's Guide* until the tourist info opened, and after acquiring a map I set off for Belgrade's top attraction, Kalemegdan Park. However, the walk was taking longer than expected and I seemed to be leaving the city, so I asked a local and he told me the park was in the other direction! He advised me to take a tram, and after following his advice I reached my destination; the public transport had a similar system to Italy, so I didn't pay. Kalemegdan features a castle, museum and zoo, as well as providing a fantastic vantage point to view the Sava and Danube confluence, so I thought it'd been worth the morning's trials and tribulations! I was relieved the staff let me leave my rucksack with them at the entrance to the zoo, as it was a hot sunny day and my back had been straining and perspiring by then; however, the zoo wasn't in the best condition and I felt sorry for the caged animals.

Returning to the centre I stopped in another park and wrote some diary. However, this was interrupted by a middle-aged man pawing me. I hadn't expected that kind of trouble in communist Yugoslavia and thought about stabbing his hand with my biro if he persisted, but his departure meant I fortunately didn't have to take that drastic step. After he left I continued writing until the light faded.

I bought a beer upon returning to the station, and sat at a table outside. A man played accordion nearby and a drunk danced to the music; his uncoordinated movements reminded me of dancing bears. The 'bear' noticed my existence after the music stopped, and approached with mischief in his eyes, but a station-worker warned him off, and he shook my hand before returning to his revelry.

I stayed at the station until it closed, and then took a bus out to the edge of the city. The location was pleasantly tranquil, idyllic even, and I soon found a nice spot hidden from the road by bushes. I was tired after all the walking, and slept well after having a #2. After the light of dawn woke me I contently lay amidst the lush vegetation, considering it my best hobo sleeping place: my own little hamlet, visible to the stars and sun but hidden from humanity.

However, I was brought back to earth with a bang after rising, as one of my trainers was covered in #2! To compound my harsh re-entry into the real world I took two wrong buses, and had to ask a local the way to the station. He needed the same tram, and we talked about the weather and football as we travelled together. I wondered why the clocks were an hour earlier than my time at the station, before a Eureka moment made me realise the clocks must have gone back; hey, I didn't

The Guns N' Roses Worker-Traveller

know they meddled with time outside the UK!

I bought a ticket for Skopje, and departed a cloudy Belgrade on the 9 a.m. train. A couple of male backpackers entered my carriage followed by two attractive females, but my hopes for a good journey were soon *shot down in flames* as a guard told us it was reserved for the police and we had to leave. I walked down the corridor and stood by a window. The females sat in a nearby compartment, and one later made conversation with me; she said they were travelling from Sweden straight to Athens, and wanted to work on an island over the winter. They had similar plans to me, and it could have been the start of something, but I think I spoilt it when I said I needed a wash, and she might have thought I meant her. Either that or she just got bored, because she went back to her friend and didn't return! To make matters worse, a ticket collector came round and took another 1400 dinars off me, pushing the price of the journey up to 5,000. The rest of the time I just took in the scenery, which was mostly flat and mundane, but the trees looked nice in their autumn colours. The weather cleared as we travelled south, and it was hot and sunny when we arrived in Skopje at about 5 p.m..

I ate the last of my provisions in the station and enquired about trains to Thessalonika for the morning. Walking into town on a bit of a low I was tempted by a bottle of coconut flavoured spirit for 2500 dinars. I resisted, but thought about travelling to Greece that night, as Skopje didn't have much to offer and I wanted to reach Athens in time for my birthday three days later. So I returned to the station and found out there was a train at 22:40, but I was just short of the 8,000 dinars needed for the ticket. I tried the exchange office in the station, asking to change a 10,000 lire note, but one of

Marc Latham

the three personnel behind the desk said they were closed. I was really pissed off with their attitude and returned to the park in an even worse mood. I calmed down through reading and writing, and then slept in a smaller park; I was quite well hidden in the dark, but woke early after the *crosstown traffic* built up.

I washed in the train station and returned to the exchange desk, but they told me to use the post office. I followed their advice, but had no luck there either, although they suggested the bank, and I eventually changed the lire there. With enough dinars to exit Yugoslavia I quickly bought a ticket to Thessalonika. The train left at 11 a.m., and I shared a compartment with three Greeks having an animated conversation. The journey was uneventful apart from stopping at the Greek border; I changed the rest of my dinars into drachmas there, and was delighted to receive another passport stamp.

After arriving in Thessalonika at about 4.30 p.m. I changed £50 at 220 drachmas to the pound. I tried to find the road south but ended up along the sea-front, not knowing if I'd got lost, or been lured by the nice scenery. After enjoying a burger and the view I found the correct road and started hitching. A short lift got me out of town before dark, and I bedded down behind a petrol station.

I started the next day with a barren spell of hitching, so when an old man advised me it would be better farther down the road I reluctantly followed his advice. I was grateful later, as the walk on an already hot morning brought me a short lift that wasn't much in itself, but it took me to a spot where I received a 150 mile lift through nice mountain scenery. The driver pointed out Mount Olympus along the way, and also shouted *malaka* at other drivers and the police a lot,

The Guns N' Roses Worker-Traveller

motioning that it meant wanker. This snippet of local knowledge led me into trouble later, as you'll find out! After the temperamental lift dropped me off I hitched from another petrol station, receiving a lift with a middle-aged man; the van had a flat tyre on the way but it didn't take long to repair. He dropped me off on a long straight road in a dry, desolate valley, with only stunning mountain scenery as a consolation. Fearing a long hiatus I started walking, but a few minutes later a camper-van stopped and took me to the edge of Athens.

The driver was a big German on his way to a geological study. He'd already picked up a Greek hitcher called Popa, who turned out to be twenty days younger than me. The van wouldn't start after cutting out while stopping for me, so the geologist flagged down a pick-up; they tied a rope between the vehicles and the local started towing us. Popa and I sat in the back of the pick-up, and as we passed a couple of laughing hitchers we motioned with our arms as if to say: *What can you do!* Then to add to the slapstick the towing rope snapped, and the local didn't return after saying he would fetch help! The geologist suggested we might be better off getting another lift, as he had night-blindness and wasn't going to drive after dark, but we hung on in there; although losing a lift all the way to Athens would have been disastrous we couldn't help creasing up when the geologist wasn't looking. After giving up on the original local the geologist went to find help, and returned with a mechanic who quickly fixed it. There was no more mechanical trouble after that, but the journey continued to be a good laugh; we mostly talked football, with the geologist informing us he supported Borussia Dortmund and Popa saying he'd played professionally with PAOK Salonika until he was nineteen, but they hadn't liked his long hair and earring.

Marc Latham

The geologist dropped us off on the edge of Athens, as he was continuing to his work-site. I paid sixty drachmas for train tickets to Popa's neighbourhood, as he was skint after failing to find apple-picking work in Volos. Approaching his house Popa asked me to wear a jumper, as he said people were wary of tattoos in Greece. His home was nice inside, and there was nobody else there when we arrived. He put the Rolling Stones on the stereo, as he was a big fan and I also liked them; we drank a couple of beers while eating chicken and fried potatoes that had been left on the stove. His parents and older brother returned later, and after introductions and more food Popa took me to meet some of his friends at a local bar. They were cool, but I felt like a bit of a spare part when Popa later fell asleep and they talked amongst themselves. After leaving, Popa took me to a park near his home, as he said his parents didn't want me to stay at their house and he couldn't find a friend to put me up. He gave me his watch and told me to call for him just before noon. I soon bedded down and slept soundly, feeling upbeat after hitching 350 miles, making it to my destination and having a cultural experience with nice people.

I felt rough after rising, but relieved to be in Athens for my 22nd birthday and with no more hitching planned for a while. Apart from paying for transport through Yugoslavia I'd completed the journey I'd planned, and was looking forward to settling into a community somewhere on Crete. After reading and writing the morning away I called for Popa as arranged. My knocking awoke him, and with nobody else home he cheerfully made us cold espresso coffee. Popa said it was okay to phone the hostel where Ross and I had arranged to meet, but when I called a man said they'd been closed four years!

The Guns N' Roses Worker-Traveller

We left to meet his friends at a clothes shop one of their parents owned, and I rode pillion with Popa on his brother's 185cc motorbike. There were four of them there, and the owner bought us pizza and coffee. We had a good laugh before Popa left to ask his mother for money to buy a ticket to Italy, and some of the others also departed. I went to a park with a couple who said they took heroin when they could afford it. The sun was hot, and it felt great to relax after all the hardship.

After the sun set we rendezvoused with Popa and the others at a bar showing live European Cup football: Olympiakos of Athens lost 2-1 to Gornik Zabrze of Poland, and went out 3-2 on aggregate. There was a lot of cheering and cursing in the bar, and watching an Athens team play while in the city was a thrill. After the game we moved to another bar, before having a smoke and drink at the shop-owner's house; I washed my hair and changed into my best jeans and *Monsters of Rock* t-shirt there. Then we drove out to a rock disco in the suburbs. I only had two beers there as it was expensive, and spent most of the time watching the Greek headbangers. I was supposed to stay with the shop-owner's son that night, but his car broke down on the way home, and as it was already 4 a.m. I ended up kipping on a park bench for a few hours. Popa was working with his brother the next day and leaving for Italy the day after, so we said goodbye after the car died and he headed home. It had been a great birthday under the circumstances, and certainly different.

After leaving my rucksack at the train station the next morning I walked round the shops and market before hiking up the Acropolis. The Parthenon architecture was impressive, and the views over the city spectacular. While I was there a torrential thunder and lightning storm engulfed the area, but I luckily found a cave to *gimme shelter*. After returning to the city in a hungry mood I was refused service at a café for no apparent reason, and then became disorientated in the city. I was worried I wouldn't reach the baggage storage before it closed at 9 p.m., so I asked a local and was kindly escorted to within view of the station. After collecting my bag with twenty minutes to spare I slept under the balcony of some flats near the station to avoid the rain.

I slept okay, and the next morning visited the old Olympic stadium, the Temple of Olympian Zeus, and the Arch of Hadrian. The exhibits were again impressive, but the weather wasn't ideal, with a cold wind blowing. After returning to the station I talked with a New Zealander who was heading home after eighteen months in Australia and Europe; he gave me his Athens map before taking a train to Patra. I slept by the same flats as the previous night but lay on the grass this time as the weather was dry. The ground was a lot softer than the previous night's concrete mattress! I revisited the Acropolis the next day, specifically to take a photo I thought I should have taken two days earlier. After that I felt there was nothing left for me in Athens and decided to leave the city a day earlier than planned. I took the train to Piraeus port, but was caught without a ticket at the other end, although the fine was only sixty drachmas!

I bought a ticket for the Crete ferry in the metro station for 1,835 drachmas, and was told we could board but it might not sail that night due to bad weather; the advice proved correct on both counts. I wasn't too bothered, as I watched *Moonlighting* in the lounge; the first English language television I'd seen since leaving home. However, after the novelty wore off I started dozing, so I bedded down afterwards. I was still sleeping

The Guns N' Roses Worker-Traveller

rough, but at least I was under a roof, among other people, and had a legitimate reason for doing it!

Pieter from Nice popped up again the next day, providing my first experience of what a small world it can be when you're on the hobo trail; ironically, he was my least favourite traveller out of those I'd met! He said there wasn't much chance of the ferry leaving that day, and later returned to say he was jumping ship. I didn't mind the waiting after my travel travails through Europe, and was quite enjoying the security and stability. I also got to see the goals from the weekend matches around Europe, which was a right bonus! At bedtime I conveniently entered the land of nod between the tables and chairs I'd been sat at during the day. The next day was groundhogish apart from talking to a Swedish traveller called Tobias who also planned to work on Crete over the winter.

The ferry finally set sail the next evening, but the relief didn't last long, as I soon discovered I'd made a big clanger when they came round for tickets: I was on the wrong boat! It really pissed me off having to pay another 1,755 drachmas after all the skimping I'd done across Europe, although I was mostly just peeved at my own ineptitude! The next morning I awoke with a crowd of people around me, and after finding my bearings realised we were entering Iraklion harbour. This also surprised me, as I'd intended going to Chania, the port on the western side of northern Crete, rather than Iraklion on the eastern half!

I left the boat with Tobias: we headed to the tourist information centre to ask about work. The woman said we shouldn't work without a permit, but was friendly enough and suggested we try Galini in the south-west, so we bought a ticket and bussed down.

Marc Latham

The journey took two hours and passed quickly, as we talked constantly. The scenery was also excellent, as we travelled through mountain passes to a picturesque coastal village. After arriving we asked a scruffy travelling couple about work; they said there wasn't any in Galini, but there was in the nearby village of Timbaki.

We decided to check out the beach before moving to Timbaki, but as we walked down some steps Tobias recognised a woman he'd met at a party in Stockholm. He started talking to Greta and a couple of Swedish friends she was travelling with: Sophia, who had long dark hair; and Toni, a medium blonde. They said they were sleeping on the beach at the far side of the bay and invited us to stay, so we decided to spend the night in Galini. I left my rucksack with the girls on the beach while Tobias rented a room. Then Tobias and I got a bus to investigate the work situation, but didn't reach our intended destination, as several worker-travellers milling about in the nearer village of Pirgos made us disembark there, thinking it was Timbaki. It was a fateful error considering what was to happen in Pirgos over the following weeks, but would staying on the bus to Timbaki have changed anything? After finding Kosta's, the Pirgos work-café, we talked to some worker-travellers about the employment situation, and received good reports. Then we had to scarper for the last bus to Galini, which we didn't know was the final one until it was about to depart.

After returning to Galini we met up with the girls and had a few beers with food; the amber-nectar tasted lush on a hot evening, and was complimented by good company and an ambient atmosphere. At the end of the night Tobias went to his room and I returned to the beach with the girls. There was a full moon and clear starry sky above, and the only sounds breaking the *still*

The Guns N' Roses Worker-Traveller

of the night below were the dulcet voices of the Swedes and the sea gently lapping against the shore. Tobias and I intended working in Pirgos the next day, but there was no early bus, so we gave it a miss. Tobias checked out of his room and moved down the beach in the morning. We thought about visiting Mires to enquire about work in the afternoon, but in the end couldn't drag ourselves away from a dreamy day of sunbathing and swimming with the girls. It turned out to be totally the right decision, as not only did we enjoy the afternoon, but we were later told there wasn't any work in Mires!

The five of us visited the village in the evening for souvlaki and beer. The girls made colourful cloth bracelets and we chatted about the usual traveller topics: Tobias was heading to Thailand for a couple of months after Europe and the Middle-East, and his portrayal of it as a cheap hedonistic paradise made me think about changing my post-Europe plans and heading east rather than west. I grew closer to Sophia early on, but then others joined us and most people started dancing, so it didn't develop in the bar. I talked to a couple of the new people most of the time: Jason and Peter from Oxford. They were in Galini on a week's holiday, and went to a disco after the bar. I returned to the beach with Sophia and slept next to her. We were the last to emerge from our sleeping bags in the morning and later walked up to the centre together. She laughed when an old woman gave me a row for washing my hair under a tap, and I just looked at them in mock disgrace! It was another beautiful day on the beach, and Greta gave me a blue, green and pink cloth bracelet.

However, the good times ended in the afternoon, as Tobias left for Israel and the girls later hitched to another beach along the coast. Tobias asked me to contact his mother if I found good work on Crete, as he'd return; I exchanged addresses and hugs with the girls. I hoped to see them all again, and especially Sophia, but never did. Jason and Peter joined us as the girls left, and stayed talking with me for an hour.

I read until dark, and then lay on the beach until going up to the centre, where I drank a beer before buying a big bottle of ouzo for 1,500 drachmas. *Bottle in hand* I walked half way up the hill leading out of the village and drank it sitting on the side of the path with some bottled water, looking down on the beach and up at the mountains and stars. After quickly downing it I bought another one, and started drinking it near the bar I'd been in; the second bottle was of course a tragic error, and the next day I couldn't remember drinking it.

I woke on the beach with a terrible hangover, a cut on my head and scratches on my face and shoulder. My rucksack was also missing. After summoning the strength to rise I walked to the village and asked about my rucksack at bars, restaurants and the police station. I had no luck, and as time passed I became worried it was the end of my journey, as my passport and traveller cheques were in the rucksack. However, as I entered the village for the umpteenth time I saw what looked like a rucksack on a seat facing the sea, and after nearing it I was absolutely chuffed to find it was mine and everything was still there.

I returned to the beach feeling relieved to have found all my stuff, but still angry with myself about how I'd behaved. I went for a swim and felt refreshed under the tepid surface. The water washed the caked blood off my head, and I'd have liked it to erase the whole experience, but the cuts and bruises were left as a lasting reminder of my recklessness, and even they didn't prevent me soon doing it again! I recuperated on the beach until after dark and then went up to the village, where I had a great view of a big bright moon coming over the mountains into another clear night sky from what I now thought of as the rucksack-seat.

I tried to piece together what happened during my *blackout*: as my last memories of the night were outside the bar, and the next clue was the finding of the rucksack on the seat, I deduced the elementary explanation was that I must have moved to the bench for the second bottle of ouzo, or sat there after finishing it, and forgot about the rucksack when I staggered to my sandy resting place.

After the thinking got a bit much I read for a while before frequenting the Jazz bar. The manager began laughing when I entered and gave me a free beer. I accepted even though I'd vowed not to drink that night, only because it would have been rude not to of course! He said I'd been in there the previous night and I was uncontrollably drunk, so an English couple now sitting in the bar had helped him handle me. So I apologised to him and joined the couple; I also said sorry to them, and they were fine about it. They said I'd been playing air-guitar the previous night and was all over the place, but I'd then moved on and they'd forgotten about me. However, after leaving the bar they saw me lying unconscious in the middle of the plaza with a bloke feeling for a pulse. The three of them took me to the bench where I'd found my rucksack, and left me there with my jumper over me. Their information meant my Sherlockian theories about what happened were way off the mark, and I filled them in on my story from the day to complete the episode. After the drink I said goodnight to everybody before returning to the beach. It was strange to be alone and sober again after having company and some great times over the previous days, and I guess it was that feeling of loss and loneliness I'd been trying to escape from the previous night.

The ouzo reverberations continued the next morning, as I realised I'd lost my watch. One of my eyes was also closed, and my head still hurt. I lazed the day away on the beach. Jason and Peter visited me in the afternoon; they sympathised with my injuries and said they *thought something like that might happen after the others left in the afternoon*. We frequented the centre for a few drinks in the evening after I hid my rucksack behind some steps. We talked quite a lot about sport, and American Football in particular, as Peter played for a team. A couple of Irish blokes they knew also joined us. One of them, Craig, was a good laugh and into Heavy Metal, with his soft perm making him resemble a slightly slimmer version of Eddie Large. At the end of the night we frequented the disco, and I was delighted to hear a *whole lotta* Metal. I talked and danced with a British woman called Amanda, while Peter accompanied her friend, and at the end of the night the four of us walked down the beach. The sky was lightening, and we anticipated a beautiful sunrise, but in the end tiredness arrived first. We walked the girls back to the centre, and I had a kiss off Amanda before she retired. I collected my rucksack and returned to my usual sleeping area, but slept behind some trees to shelter from the rising sun.

Peter hired a pedalo during the afternoon, and me and Craig went along with him. We couldn't steer it properly so it was a right laugh, spending most of the time going round in circles with Craig holding on behind us snorkelling! Craig lent me his walkman and AC/DC's *Who Made Who* tape in the evening, and it was great to

The Guns N' Roses Worker-Traveller

hear the tracks again; especially *Ride On*, with its melancholy lyrics reflecting my psyche at the time. We also had a good conversation before he left to meet the others for a meal. I'd declined the offer as I thought it would be expensive, and was worried about running down my finances in a week I was supposed to be working. Craig waved me over after they'd eaten, and I joined them for a few drinks, but the evening never really took off, as everybody was still recovering from the previous night.

I awoke desperate for a #2, and as it was a bit early for a morning dip I rushed inland. Relieved to be emptied of waste I spent a few hours relaxing on the beach, and started reading *Enemy Mine*; about a human and an alien who meet as enemies after shooting each other down in a futuristic dog-fight, and then have to co-operate together on a hostile planet. I'd packed ready to go in the afternoon when Amanda turned up. She told me the others were on the next beach, so after we'd finished chatting I said goodbye to her and joined them. I ended up staying ages, and had a great laugh; I also read a *Daily Mirror* they had, and gave Craig my *Easyriders* book. We exchanged addresses and wished each other luck before I left them and Galini. I hadn't found any work, but I'd had some good times and a mini-holiday. I'd tell my future friends in Pirgos how nice Galini was, but I never returned.

After bussing it to Pirgos I ate some bread and cheese by the side of a restaurant until the owner appeared and sent me packing. It wasn't a good start, and things would get much worse! I relocated to steps overlooking the sea, and finished the food as the sun set in the distance. After moving to Kosta's and sitting at a table of card players a friendly Dutchman called Ferry gave me advice about the work situation. He also bought me a couple of beers without even asking if I wanted one! He had a Greek girlfriend, Nadia, and said locals had given him hassle about it. We also talked about the Amsterdam music scene, and he said he'd met John Lydon and Nina Hagen there. After Kosta's we moved to a couple of bars called Zorba's and Remezzos; there was a *Platoon* poster on the wall in Remezzos and *World-Wide Live* played on the stereo. At the end of the night they escorted me to the beach before leaving for their squat. I'd moved villages, but was back on the beach!

Dawn awoke me and I frequented Kosta's. There were already a few worker-travellers resident and I got talking to Kenny, a twenty-three year old Briton with a kid from a short marriage. It wasn't long before a farmer approached us looking for a worker, and in the end took us both. He drove us out to some greenhouses and provided my first worker-traveller employment: 1,250 drachmas for a morning of picking and bagging cucumbers. It was hot inside the greenhouses but the work was light and steady.

Kenny took me to some half-built houses where he and some others were dossing after we got dropped off in Pirgos. I washed myself with a hose outside before we returned to Kosta's and spent a few hours drinking beer and playing cards: the beer, cards, saloon-bars, transient work, ghost town atmosphere, apparent lawlessness and our scruffiness brought the Wild West analogies back to mind.

We got more work later, on a job that became progressively more difficult as it developed. In the end we were loading and unloading crates of cucumbers six high onto a lorry and into a factory. I dropped one load, and locals shouted at us a couple of times, but it wasn't

The Guns N' Roses Worker-Traveller

too bad. We worked five hours and received 1,500 drachmas each, so it worked out at just over a pound an hour; a lot less than you'd get for similar work in the UK!

After returning to Kosta's we were joined by a geezer called Bob, who spun tall tales about his travels and some plain rubbish, like claiming that Crete was as far south as South Africa! Then we had a beer and omelette in Yanni's, collected our rucksacks from Kosta's before it closed at 9, and had a few drinks in Zorba's. At the end of the night we returned to the house and bedded down in what looked like the living-room.

Kenny and Bob woke me at 6:30 and we frequented Kosta's. We didn't get employed, but weren't too bothered as it was another sunny day. We spent the morning playing kaluki, a variation of rummy played a lot in the café, and hitched to Timbaki in the afternoon. However, most places were closed, so we soon returned to Pirgos. We spent the night in Zorba's, joining a big crowd of worker-travellers partying to good music. I talked with quite a few new people, including a Yorkshireman called Rick who'd just arrived from another town on Crete; a Yugoslav named Davo who slept at our squat; and a Greek-South African called Saul who'd recently returned from Africa. One worker-traveller bet another he could burn a hole through a hundred drachma note pressed against his skin, but ended up just burning himself. I began to feel settled in my first community away from home.

In the morning a farmer approached Kenny and me saying he wanted one person for a job. A Scottish guy called Hamish said he had a job for me later so I let K go, but the other work later fell through, and I was left jobless. My bad work day was made complete later when a farmer needed five workers and I lost a toss of the coin with an Irish bloke called Jimmy for the last place. So I stayed in the café all day, and passed the time playing cards, draughts and backgammon. I later returned to the house and cooked some spaghetti, but typical of my day the gas ran out half way through, so I ate the pasta with cold tinned tomatoes despite it being quite crunchy. I wouldn't say it was a culinary delight, but it was edible! Back at Kosta's, Kenny pissed me off even more when he returned 3,000 drachmas richer!!

However, my luck changed later when a farmer asked Kosta about workers for the next day and he recommended Kenny and me; we eagerly agreed, although we didn't know much about the job. I was eating toast and marmalade in Kosta's the next morning when the farmer turned up. He was accompanied by two women, and one of them drove us out to some greenhouses. They gave us protective clothing, and showed us that we were supposed to collect pruned rose branches in plastic sheets and take them out to a fire. We sometimes had to carry the cuttings above our heads to stop them catching on the other branches, as some of the alleys were quite narrow, but it was generally quite comfortable work. We also had an impressive lunch of bean soup, bread, salad, small fish, an apple, cucumber and a big glass of wine. I didn't feel like working after that and slowed down for a while, but they seemed happy with our work and asked us back the next day. We were paid 2,700 drachmas and that was to become the standard day's wage. They also returned us to Kosta's, where I read a *Times* newspaper somebody had left; it reported that Kiss was up from 12 to 5 in the charts with *Crazy, Crazy Nights*, and Bruce Springsteen's *Tunnel of Love* had entered the album chart at number one.

The Guns N' Roses Worker-Traveller

Work went to schedule the next day and we finished collecting the cuttings in the afternoon. We hadn't known if that was the end of the job, and were relieved to be given clippers and shown how to cut stems; we roughly cut them to chest height, and the women followed us tidying them up. At the end of the day they said there was no work on Sunday, but there was on Monday. As we were off work the next day we planned to visit Galini in the night, and I got quite excited about it, but anticipation turned to disappointment in the evening, as the bus didn't turn up and we stayed in Pirgos! It was a good night nonetheless, with a bigger crowd than normal in Remezzos and Zorba's, and I was one of the last to leave.

We went over Kosta's later than usual in the morning, not really bothered about working, but then a woman arrived needing two workers for a job in a restaurant. Saul and Kenny took it, and I was angry with the latter because he'd taken the previous job offered between us; it was the start of a pattern that lasted throughout. I spent the day between café and house, playing cards most of the time. Kenny was drunk off restaurant wine when he returned in the evening, and brought a beer into Kosta's. This obviously pissed the eponymous proprietor off, although he didn't object. We frequented Remezzos after Kosta's closed, and I quarrelled with Kenny about him taking jobs ahead of me. It became quite heated for a while but calmed down by the end of the night, although I was still seething inside. I talked with Rick for most of the night, preferring his company and more interested in his conversation; he said he'd been away from Britain for eighteen months since getting divorced, and had recently been living in the famous Matala caves elsewhere on Crete. During the night we heard a British girl had walked through a pane of glass at the Kalipso bar thinking it was an open door, but had escaped unscathed.

We pruned roses again the next day, and forgot about the previous night's argument. Kenny was hung-over anyway, so I thought that was punishment enough! Bob and Hamish lightened the mood back at the café, talking about their day picking cucumbers. Meeting up with the others at the end of the work-day was something I always looked forward to, as I saw it as a kind of tribal gathering, with the individual members all returning with stories from their day to entertain and inform the others.

However, the smiles were wiped off our faces later that evening when a car pulled up outside and three policemen entered to check passports. I'd been leaving mine in my rucksack, but luckily had it on me that night and didn't have any problems; but it was a different story for Jimmy, as he'd overstayed his three month visa, and they took him and another worker with them. It was a bit of a shock after the previously easygoing experience I'd had on Crete, and was a sign of things to come.

I couldn't find my trainers in the morning, although everything else was in place. After starting to panic I eventually found them under Frank's cranium; he'd been paralytic the night before and used them as a pillow! Frank had scratches on his face from a fall, and I later found out he'd pissed on a couple while they were asleep in the house. The morning back on track, we were picked up from Kosta's as usual and spent another day with a *whole lotta roses*. We worked on our own some of the time, and after lunch I napped under some decent rays on a warm afternoon.

The Guns N' Roses Worker-Traveller

Jimmy was back when we returned to Kosta's. He said they'd given him two days to get a visa, and five others had already been deported. There were also a few new British faces there: a Metaller called Simon, who had a similarly dark scruffy look to Kenny and me, and three girls from Accrington; two tallish blondes called Michelle and Margot, and a smaller dark haired one named Tanya. The police activity and influx of new blood brought a fresh excitement to town, and it turned into quite a mad night at Zorba's: Jimmy got paralytic and aggressive, there was an altercation between a worker and a German tourist at the entrance, and Kenny cracked the screen of the Pac-man machine after getting eaten. I didn't have much to drink but thought it was the best night I'd had in Pirgos! Kenny, Simon and a couple of others took a crate of beer to the beach afterwards, but I didn't fancy it and went home. They brought the leftover beers back to the house, and we necked them for brekkie in the morning.

Another day on the roses followed. We took it easy as we'd nearly completed our current task and thought we'd be finished once we had. Kenny was hung-over from the previous night and had the kip after lunch, with me on look-out duty. We still finished all the work we knew about, but they asked us back the next day. After work I updated the diary while talking with the others until football came on television: Panathinaikos of Athens beat Juventus of Turin 1-0 at home in the first leg of one of the European cups. After the game I went to Zorba's with Kenny, Bob and Simon. It was another good night, with rounds of beers followed by ouzo. I talked quite a lot with Michelle, a fellow Metaller; she was working alternate nights behind the bar at Zorba's with Margot.

Kenny slept in the next day and Rick worked

instead. We cleared the plastic and hay from the greenhouses. I'd worried that that was the end of the job, but they asked us to bring an extra worker for the next day. Back at Kosta's we sat with Simon, who said he'd slept until lunchtime. Simon read his book, Rick read Simon's *Mega Metal* magazine, and I wrote my diary. I also let them read a passage of it as they were curious about what I found to write about!

Then Jimmy entered and said the police were over at our house, so Simon and I rushed over to check it out. The police weren't there when we arrived, but Kenny was. He said they'd kicked him in the back to wake him and told him we all had to leave, but our stuff was okay. So we took our rucksacks with us, and continued the discussion over a few drinks in Zorba's, while listening to Simon's Iron Maiden, Dio, and Metallica tapes on their stereo. Simon was skint, so I lent him 1,000 drachmas. I played draughts with Michelle and we had a good chat, but then the beer ran out and we were forced onto ouzo! I remembered my mind becoming nicely free and jumbled, with time no longer relevant, inhibitions and worry long gone, and the pursuit of euphoria everything.

I woke on the beach. The sun was scorching so I guessed it must be around midday. My head hurt and there was blood on it, so I knew I'd done something quite serious to myself before I'd even recovered from the night in Galini. The physical pain was therefore compounded by mental anguish, as I'd let alcohol fuck me up again. There were rocks and pebbles all around me, so I thought I must have fallen on them from the adjacent cliff, which was twenty feet high. The searing sun eventually forced me to rise, although my head was still reluctant. I groggily walked to the left along the beach and up some steps visible from below. However,

The Guns N' Roses Worker-Traveller

as I neared the top I saw it was a dead-end, and as I couldn't face hiking anywhere else I returned to the beach and found a small cave that sheltered me from the UV. However, it didn't protect me from the flies, and I was awake most of the time trying to stop them feeding off the blood on my head; I told you it was purgatory didn't I! I had to tolerate the flies for a few hours, until I could muster the energy to leave. It was late in the afternoon by then, as the heat of the sun began to relent. I made my way to the right over rocks and through the sea, and then up a path leading back into the living world.

I visited Zorba's first and got some toiletries from my rucksack, which was still there from the previous night. Although I didn't know exactly where I'd awoken on the beach I thought I must have fallen off the cliff behind Zorba's, as it was used as an extra cubicle if the toilet was occupied; although, as in Galini, I didn't really have a clue what happened. After washing back at the house I walked over to Kosta's, seeing my face in a van mirror on the way; it was a real mess, with my right eye completely closed and deep scratches around it. I could also feel cuts on top of my head, and my right leg, ribs and wrist also hurt. I perceptively guessed I must have fallen onto my right side!

Kosta was visibly shocked by my appearance when I walked into the café, while Margot and Michelle could hardly look at the injuries. They got me some antiseptic liquid and cotton-wool, but didn't want to do the job themselves as it was too gross. They said we'd drunk a few bottles of ouzo the previous night, and Simon and Bob nearly had a fight in the bar about whose round it was. Simon and I left together and then they heard Simon had been taken to Iraklion hospital with a suspected broken arm after falling down some steps near the beach.

After a while my head started aching again, and I went to sleep on Kosta's table until a few of the lads came back from work. Hamish had been on the roses job instead of me, and Bob and Jimmy offered me light work with them the next day. They suggested I get a room for the night, and recommended a cheap hotel. I made my way over to it after a while and asked about a bed, but they kept me waiting for ages and said it was 1,000 drachmas a night, so I didn't take it. As I returned to Kosta's I started getting nauseous, so I entered a half-built building that looked empty. I didn't have my rucksack or sleeping bag with me, so I just lay on the concrete with the temperature just about warm enough to tolerate. However, I didn't sleep for ages and just lay there, not knowing what time of night it was. In the end I dropped off for some kind of prolonged sleep.

I was awoken in the morning by some worker-travellers who'd also slept in the house. I reached Kosta's by 7, and joined some of the others. Hamish didn't mind going to work with Jimmy, so I worked on the roses again. Our job for the day was putting dirt from the greenhouse in little bags. It was nice and easy, and we were surprised when the farmer asked us to bring an additional worker with us on Monday. After returning to Pirgos the others went for a meal at Yanni's. It was Saturday night, but I didn't feel like partying! Instead, I updated my diary, and later had my first sustenance of the day: bread and jam, yoghurt and a coke. It wasn't safe to sleep in the house after the police raid, so I moved to a derelict restaurant called El Greco; Rick already slept there, and Bob joined us the next night. The temperature had turned colder, or at least it felt that way to me, and I wore my jacket inside the sleeping bag. Four new worker-travellers had arrived from the UK a few days earlier, but two had already returned. I was quite envious, as it wasn't much fun working out in weather that felt like winter in the UK, and then sitting in a café without heating or comfortable seats in the night, and especially when your head was half caved in! I was thinking about going to Israel in a few weeks, as it sounded much warmer from the reports I'd received.

Kenny and Michelle hitched up to see Simon on Monday, so Bob came with us on the roses job. Kenny returned with a couple of English papers in the evening, but Michelle stayed in hospital with Simon; he was due for an operation on Wednesday. The farmer wanted Bob instead of Kenny the next day, and losing the job pissed K off; it was the start of what could be termed the War of the Roses or the Cold War, as K didn't talk with B for a few days. I felt better on Wednesday, and could do more, although my ribs still hurt if I breathed in deeply. We stopped off in Timbaki on the way home, and it was a bit more exciting on a normal day; I was thrilled to find some new Heavy Metal records in a music shop, before we adjourned to the Raki bar to shoot some pool. I ate loads of snacks while playing, and followed it with double egg and chips. I also had my first beer since the fall. It was becoming a good evening, and after returning to Pirgos in a taxi we frequented Zorba's. A few of the others got drunk, but I stuck to two beers. Kenny and Margot had hitched up to see Simon during the day, and Michelle returned with them; Simon hadn't had his operation, and it was now set for the following Monday.

It was warmer the next day, and doing the new job made it more enjoyable than before. Life was improving after the low of the previous week...but it wasn't to last! At lunch-time we had a tasty meat and rice dish, but my enjoyment was curtailed upon finding a head. I made out the teeth first and thought it was a rat, but then realised it must be rabbit. It was pretty awful at the time, but we had a good laugh about it. That set the tone for the afternoon, and we frequently clowned around; the family didn't look happy when they saw us!

Kenny started talking to Bob again in the evening, which was a relief to everybody. We drank a yellowish Greek wine called retsina for the first time, and were feeling quite sloshed after a relatively small amount. I chatted with Tanya at Zorba's, and she helped me write a letter to Simon, as I couldn't hold the biro properly with my damaged right hand; Michelle was going to deliver it. I got pissed by the end of the night and couldn't remember retiring to my bag-bed in El Greco. The next thing I recalled was being woken in the middle of the night by Rick approaching me, and then realising Bob was already beside me. It was initially quite shocking, but then I noticed torrential rain was seeping through the numerous holes in the ceiling, and I was sleeping in the middle of the only dry spot in the room!

On Saturday morning our boss told us there was no work until Monday, so I decided to make a weekend of it. I started off with my first #2 since the fall nine days earlier, and then visited Timbaki with Bob, Kenny and Hamish. We had a good day there, starting with the usual big meal, pool and beers. Then we met some worker-travellers we vaguely knew from Pirgos, and sat outside a restaurant on the square drinking wine together. An older guy called Trev kept us entertained with some hilarious stories from his life, although he had a row off a local for climbing on a table while telling one. He ended up comatose under a Raki bar pool table after we'd reconvened there for the more booze and pool.

The Guns N' Roses Worker-Traveller

We returned to Pirgos later and finished off at the Zorba's Halloween party, which was packed out and a good laugh.

I lost my memory during the night, but Bob filled me in on the highlights and lowlights when we awoke. I was relieved to hear I hadn't misbehaved too badly, although he said I was flicking nuts at Tanya; she'd started working behind the bar in Zorba's instead of Michelle. He also said we witnessed a car crash while walking home, but I didn't remember anything about it!

I must have let my relatively good behaviour go to my head, because within an hour I was on the retsina outside Zorba's. I wasn't alone though, as there was a crowd of people carrying on from the night before on a warm sunny day. It was a great laugh, with everybody in high spirits after we started drinking jugs of grassi; a home-made wine that's cheaper and more potent than retsina! I hadn't gone back on the ouzo since the fall, but was drinking my way up the ladder of strength. Hamish provided the best laugh of the day by falling off his chair!

I lent Kenny 2,000 drachmas in the evening, and got closer to Tanya in Zorba's; giving her my cloth-bracelet after she said she liked it. At the end of the night I walked her home and we had a bit of a kiss. The girls were staying at the house of a local Cretan they met when they arrived: Talon. Tanya was a good laugh and attractive, although I had initially been more interested in Michelle. I was chuffed to have got off with her, but didn't know at the time it was the beginning of the end for me in Pirgos.

I still felt pissed in the morning and therefore didn't feel hung-over; in fact, I was on a high after a great weekend and a noticeable improvement in the weather. We even had a kick-about in work at lunchtime after finding a ball. Rick and Bob were humorously slagging each other off all day and it was a good laugh, with the banter generally revolving around Rick being older than us, and Bob, well, being Bob! They also poked fun at me about Tanya, but I quite enjoyed it, as it was nice to have a bit of female interest again.

We played kaluki in Kosta's after work, followed by more boozing in Zorba's. Tanya was there and we continued flirting, but she dropped a bit of a bombshell after Bob left, telling me he'd brought her a rose back from work. After I'd helped him make peace with Kenny I thought it was totally two-faced, and especially as he'd been teasing me about Tanya but hadn't said anything about taking her a rose. Apart from talking to Tanya I spent most of my time with Rick and Hamish, and had a great laugh with them. Davo asked me if he could borrow 5,000 drachmas but I turned him down, as I'd already lent thousands out and didn't know him that well; however, as things turned out he deserved it more than those I had lent money. I walked Tanya home again, and we sat outside the house talking and kissing. She also had a look in my diary to see what I'd written about her.

Bob woke me in the morning and I didn't bother confronting him about the rose, as I thought his behaviour was sad, and Tanya wasn't interested in him. It rained while we worked, and after the family saw me skiving a couple of times they said they only wanted the other three from then on; I wasn't too bothered, as I had a decent amount of money. We got dropped off in Timbaki again and had the usual meal, pool and booze. There was no taxi around at the end of the night, so we walked back to Pirgos. I lost my memory back in

The Guns N' Roses Worker-Traveller

Zorba's, but was later told I was drinking retsina faster than Rick and Bob drank beer, and Bob and I had a scuffle with two locals after I called them malakas (remember my first hitch in Greece teaching me that!) for pestering Tanya and Margot. I left with Tanya, Margot and Kenny; the girls showed us to a house near theirs, as downpours had saturated El Greco. However, I didn't settle there, and after getting lost I slept in another half-built building. While I was wandering around, Talon saw me near his house and shouted at me, but didn't say anything after coming close.

I awoke without my day-bag in the morning, and couldn't remember where I'd left it. So I was relieved when Kenny brought it into Kosta's; he said I'd left it in the house the girls had shown us and he'd slept. After remaining jobless we washed with the hose at the original squatting house. I scrubbed my hair and changed my clothes for the first time in a week. Partially cleansed, we began drinking retsina with some of the others. Tanya wasn't happy I was drinking so early, as she didn't like my paralytic persona. I couldn't remember much after a few bottles, but was later told I was talking to myself and playing air-guitar to Bon Jovi's *Living on a Prayer*; no doubt providing the best laugh of the day for the others!

I must have stopped drinking in my stupor, as I sobered enough to remember watching the second leg of Juventus versus Panathinaikos, which was 0-0 at half-time when Kosta's closed. Bob and I tried to find somewhere to watch the second half, but Yanni's was closed and they wouldn't let us in anywhere else. So we returned to Kosta's and watched the game through the window until Kosta's wife asked us in. Kosta and another local were the only other ones there. It was a great second half, with Juventus winning 3-2 but

Panathinaikos going through on away goals after their 1-0 home win.

I frequented Zorba's after the game, and mainly talked with Kenny and Rick until walking Tanya home at the end of the night. We had a nice time again, but she asked if I loved her, and said that if I was only after sex I shouldn't bother. I slept well at a dried out El Greco, but felt rough the next day despite sleeping in. Having risen, I shuffled over to Kosta's and joined Rick at a table. I had toast and coffee while reading a *Daily Mirror* left on the table. It was a quiet start to what promised to be a boring day, but appearances can be deceiving, and for me it turned out to be the calm before a cyclone!

Rick left and I started updating my diary, before being joined by Kenny, Tanya and Margot; T and M said they were moving out of Talon's house, and then he entered and asked to speak to me outside. I suspected there was trouble afoot from his disposition, and boy, was I not wrong. I took my jacket off before following him around the corner of the café. He attacked me but I evaded his punches, and caught him with a sweet left hook that instantly bled his nose; my right hand was unusable due to the fall. Then he grabbed me and it developed into a wrestling match, with both of us falling on the floor. As we struggled for supremacy in the dust and dirt I saw other locals wielding sticks, so I relaxed my ambitions from winning to survival; I'd heard stories of travellers falling foul of locals, with the resulting murders, rapes and beatings by civilians and police reminiscent of lynch mobs in the Wild West. I covered up and was being hit by Talon and some of the others until Davo, who was a big bloke, pushed in and stopped it. I returned to Kosta's and sat where I had been, but Talon and some of the others followed me in and tried to get at me; they had to be restrained until eventually

The Guns N' Roses Worker-Traveller

leaving.

The two girls, Kenny and I decided to leave Pirgos as soon as possible. K and I collected our rucksacks from Zorba's, while the girls fetched their stuff from Talon's house. We met at Zorba's and walked towards Kosta's, but Talon and some locals blocked the road with pick-ups; he'd told Margot it was all over when they were at his house, but as we neared the Cretan line he attacked me. I didn't see any point in enflaming the situation, so just covered up again. Talon wrestled me to the floor and another local started hitting me with a stick, but Talon chased him off. This might sound like Talon had taken pity on my poor battered bones, but it's my guess that he didn't want anybody to steal his thunder, as he then continued to assault me. As he hit me he asked if it hurt. I said no at first, but he kept up the verbal and physical assault, so in the end I answered yes, as he obviously wasn't going to stop until then. The magic word did the trick, and the beating ceased. The locals left, with Margot shouting at them hysterically, and Tanya also crying.

After regaining our composure we walked up to Kosta's. The bus to Iraklion thankfully arrived soon after; the four of us boarded, paid our fares, and escaped purgatory! I thought of returning like the anti-hero in *High Plains Drifter* for some time after that, but never got round to it. I was angry about having to take the beating, but was also relieved to have evaded serious injury or worse; although it hadn't done my previous injuries any good, and my head had started bleeding again! We hardly said a word on the bus, and everybody seemed in a mild state of shock.

After arriving in Iraklion we looked for Simon and Michelle in the hospital, but the receptionist told us they'd left earlier that day. So we found a hotel room and ate some mushroom soup and bread I had. We rested until the evening, and then went over to a bar in Alliance Square for a few drinks, spending most of the time trying to make sense of the day's events. After returning to the hotel, Kenny slept on the single bed while I shared the double with the girls; we all used sleeping-bags, as there was only one blanket for each bed. It was nice waking next to Tanya in the morning, and we snoozed for a while.

We visited the British consul after rising; the girls thought it might have a contact number for Michelle, while Kenny tried to get some money, but neither was successful. We also tried the tourist police about Michelle, but again drew a blank. So the girls decided they'd have to return to Pirgos, although Tanya dreaded the thought. The decision made, and best wishes exchanged, the girls boarded the midday bus, planning to hitch back with Michelle before it got dark.

Kenny and I visited the American Express office to collect mail I'd had sent there from family and friends. We read the letters in a bar and they lifted my spirits. Then we bought some food and ate it back in our room, before K slept. I read my letters again, and the newspaper cuttings that came with them, before updating my diary; this of course took ages! I was obviously pissed off about recent events, and wrote the only reason I didn't go straight to Israel was Tanya, but the situation was to take a surprising twist over the following days.

K woke briefly, but the girls hadn't returned from Pirgos when I bedded down. We were quite worried when there was still no sign of them in the morning, but they returned an hour after we rose. They said they'd

The Guns N' Roses Worker-Traveller

worked in Zorba's and stayed with Margaret. They'd seen Talon and he'd apologised, and said that it was okay for me to return without further hassle, but not Kenny; and apparently I'd broken Talon's nose and it needed surgery, which cheered me up no end. They'd also found Simon and Michelle, and they were coming up later that day.

K phoned the British consul about being skint after we checked out of the hotel, and was given an appointment for the following Monday. Simon and Michelle arrived in the afternoon. when Simon saw my injuries he said *I warned you not to quarrel with the locals*, but I replied that most of the damage came from the fall. However, there was also a bit of a conspiracy about my plunge, with Talon and other locals under suspicion.

Once we'd caught up with each other and settled into the old friendship we left our rucksacks at an Irish pub and spent the afternoon on the beach. We returned to the bar in the evening and I had double eggs on toast, followed by two plates of chips with tons of tomato sauce. There was live music on, and an electric guitarist played stonking covers of classic rock songs. I sat next to Tanya, with the others in a semi-circle around us, and the place full of worker-travellers. It made for a warm atmosphere, and having escaped purgatory I felt the relief and security shown by fictional characters that survive ordeals and make it back to their own, although there was also the feeling that it wasn't over, and the monster might reappear before the end! But no monsters appeared, and the night was thoroughly enjoyable. We ended it on the beach, and I slept next to T.

We kissed before sleeping and after waking,

which was again heart-warming. The six of us dozed and talked for a while as the sun rose, until someone started cutting grass near us. We packed and left, intending to eat, but when we couldn't find anything open we decided to hitch to Chania; five of us were leaving straight away and Kenny would follow after going to the consul in the morning.

Margot and T set off first, followed by Michelle and Simon, and then me. However, when I started walking out of town after saying goodbye to K it wasn't long before I came across the other four; they said there'd been no sign of a lift and they were returning to town. I joined them, and after reaching the centre we frequented an ice-cream parlour. Simon and I sat outside with our vanilla ice-creams while the girls talked inside.

We knew they were pissed-off about the situation, but still didn't expect the bombshell they delivered after rejoining us: they said they were returning to their jobs in Pirgos because they were skint. We exchanged hugs and kisses, said goodbye, and they left us a bit stunned. However, it wasn't long before Tanya and Michelle returned, telling us they hadn't wanted to leave, and it was Margot's idea. Michelle then went to find Margot, and also brought Kenny back, after bumping into him; the gang of desperados was reformed for another day! Our future was still undecided, but we had a good laugh about it over lunch and a beer.

We later paid 250 drachmas to enter the cinema, and watched both the 8 p.m. and 10 p.m. showings of *Predator*; we sat in the balcony for the first and moved downstairs for the second. I sat next to T in both, and we talked about our pasts and got closer, which was quite ironic considering we'd part the next day. The others slept through most of the second show, and after leaving we spent our last night together in a small park outside the bus station.

K went to the consul in the morning hoping for a sizeable hand-out, but only received 2,500 drachmas. The other four were also broke, and decided that if they didn't get some money soon they'd have to return to Pirgos. So K and I opted to leave for Chania straight away, as he needed to find work before his money ran out. It meant splitting with T, which was a shame, but the possibility of them returning to Pirgos had swung my decision away from her. We sat in the park for a while, and Margot took a photo of T and me with my camera. After saying goodbye to the others T walked with K and me for 200 yards. We kissed and said our last farewell on Crete, after telling each other we'd hopefully meet again; a wish that was to be briefly fulfilled in Israel.

K and I bought a ticket to Chania for 900 drachmas and travelled across the north coast; it was a gloomy and uneventful three hour journey, both inside and outside the bus. Darkness had descended by the time we arrived, but we declined the offer of a 1,000 drachma room and headed towards the Old Harbour. As we entered the area a British beggar requested twenty drachmas, which wasn't a good sign! We asked him where the work-café was, and he showed us the Green Bar and Costa's opposite each other. We had a walk round and found somewhere to doss down for later before frequenting the Green Bar, where Kenny got the beers in with his consul money. The gloom lifted for us a little later, after a German we got talking to called Nobby invited us to stay at his house.

We bought a bottle of ouzo on the way, and after

entering the house met a few people drinking wine on the kitchen floor; we started chatting with them about Chania life hoping for positivity, but an English bloke called Jake reckoned the work situation was generally quite tight. After finishing our booze, Kenny and I found a cheap restaurant, where we bought a pasta meal and also finished the left-overs from the next table. We had a bit of difficulty finding our way back to Nobby's house, but made it in the end. The others had fallen asleep by the time we returned and we bedded down next to them. It was nice and warm after the previous two nights outdoors, but there was no Tanya, and I would regret choosing to travel with Kenny in the following weeks.

The photo of Tanya and me

The Guns N' Roses Worker-Traveller

Chapter 3

Beach and Cave Life through Christmas to the Shores of the Middle-East: middle and late Crete, Athens and Cyprus

It was dark and I was on a beach, but I didn't know how I'd arrived or where I was. It was the second morning of the new start, and I'd already fallen back into my old ways!

On the first morning Kenny and I were awoken by Nobby and went over Costa's with him. Jake arrived later but got work before us. As time passed and my hopes for employment dwindled I relaxed my 'Mister Employable' stance and started catching up on the diary, but then an old army jeep pulled up and a local offered us work. We of course jumped at the chance and into the vehicle. Like hitch-hiking, worker-travelling provides extreme highs and lows, and you can be transported from a sense of despair and resignation to euphoria and expectation in a matter of minutes. This was one of those times, and from facing another day of dreary poverty one moment we were now driving through sunny streets with the wind in our faces, and with the prospect of earning our keep for the day or more. This time, the job turned out to be really sound, but not very lucrative. After driving to a factory, we taped up boxes containing ceramics and loaded them onto a lorry. The work lasted a couple of hours and I received 1,000 drachmas pay, which was better than expected for the time and difficulty. Kenny got another 250, as he unloaded the boxes at the airport after I got dropped off in town. After meeting up with K again at Costa's we walked into town and noticed some pretty local women around; a *sight for sore eyes* after Pirgos!

After a circuit of the centre we returned to the Old Harbour and sat with Jake and the others. We were buoyant after the promising morning, and invigorated by new people and surroundings. So after a beer and hearing about a nearby shop that stocked grassi we decided to get pissed! A one and a half litre bottle set us back 150 drachmas, but didn't last long, and once downed was followed by another. We drank the second talking life, with our legs dangling over the harbour edge; *sitting on the dock of the bay* comes to mind! However, I couldn't remember anything after the second bottle, and the next I knew was coming to my senses on the aforementioned beach.

I felt *dazed and confused* after coming to my senses, so I just bedded down between some boats. After waking later with a clearer head I realised the beach was a couple of miles west of the Old Harbour area, and walked back to Nobby's house. The weather reflected my state of mind on the hike: murky drizzle. Nobby was leaving for work when I arrived. Kenny had already departed and there was a new bloke sleeping on the floor. I slept through the day until Kenny returned in the afternoon; he'd had a couple of hours work and filled me in on the previous night. Apparently we frequented a restaurant and he bought me a souvlaki, but I squashed it; then he'd wanted to leave, but I wouldn't budge from the table and fell asleep, so he left and that was the last he saw of me.

I was relieved to have survived the escapade unscathed, and had a quiet night. Kenny repaid me 500 drachmas and we had a couple of beers and food before returning to the house. K slept but I was still wide awake after kipping all day, so I read until Nobby returned with a few drunk people. I didn't want to get involved in any conversation so I tried to sleep, but the lights were on and they kept falling over me when they came into the kitchen, so I remained awake until they bedded down.

It rained during the night and the seats outside the Green Bar were wet the next morning, so we stood waiting for inspection, like soldiers on parade. K and I didn't really expect to get employed, but then a Geordie came along and said he had work for us. A Londoner called Tony and two Greeks also came with us, and the job only took twenty minutes. We carried a boiler into the basement of a building, with the Greeks taking most of the weight. We each received 750 drachmas, a beer and two packets of cigarettes, so that paid for our day and a little more. I gave my cigarettes to Kenny.

K and I later ate at a cheap restaurant, and Tony and his girlfriend Joanna were there, along with a Scot and an Israeli; they offered us some retsina and I had a glass or two. Tony said he was an ex drug addict and current alcoholic. He'd been in the US for a couple of years and was now waiting for money from the UK to return home. The Scot had also travelled to the US and they tried to outdo each other with tales from the Deep South. They also lauded a resort on the southern coast of Crete called Paleohora, and Kenny and I thought we'd try it in a few days, as there didn't seem enough work in Chania to escape Nobby's floor. After leaving, Kenny and I returned to the Green Bar. We saw *Police Academy IV* was playing at a cinema and planned to watch it the next night, but didn't know at the time we wouldn't even be in Chania.

After we didn't get work the next morning Kenny decided to try begging. I left him to it and went over the ferry terminal to ask about my Athens-Chania ticket, but as expected they said it expired after the missed voyage and I couldn't get a refund. I returned to the Green Bar and met K there. He said he'd received 650 drachmas begging, but hated it. It had been a depressing morning, and was the final nail in the coffin for Chania; we decided to leave for Paleohora earlier than planned.

After collecting our rucksacks from the house we made our way to the bus station and bought a ticket for 460 drachmas. En route we'd picked small oranges off a tree, but when we tried them they were really sour, so we chucked the rest. Chania to Paleohora was a two hour journey over mountainous terrain, with similar scenery to my first north-south journey with Tobias, although the atmosphere was totally different; rather than the conversation, excitement and optimism of the first journey there was a silent desperation reminiscent of the final journey in *Midnight Cowboy*!

Paleohora made a good first impression, and we headed straight for one of the beaches. After reading a *Daily Mirror* we'd bought in Chania from back to front while soaking up some decent UV we returned to the village and asked a grizzled bloke outside Vangeli's café where the work-café was; he replied he was sitting outside it! We talked for a while, and Adam said there hadn't been much work but it could pick up any time. Then he showed us where other travellers were camped, with a dozen tents erected on the edge of the main beach under some trees. We thanked him and put my tent up next to the others, before eating bread and cheese through the sunset.

We frequented Vangeli's in the evening and I

The Guns N' Roses Worker-Traveller

updated my diary while talking with Adam, a woman called Vanessa and a long-haired balding bloke called Harry. Harry said he'd lived in my area for three years, and he knew a few of my friends from the counter-culture scene when I named them. When Kenny and I returned to the beach we saw there were a couple of fires lit, with travellers playing guitars around them, so we joined one group; the people seemed nice and were from all over the world.

The next morning we awoke early and hopeful, but there wasn't much activity and we didn't work. Kenny returned to the tent and slept most of the day, while I hung around the café all morning. I talked with an Ethiopian for a while, and also started a new diary book; by the time it was full I'd written *Diary of a Madman* on the front cover in not too original fashion; *NFL – Nice Fucking Life*, after the Anthrax song, and *Sweet Home_?* influenced by Lynyrd Skynyrd. I also wrote *I've lived it so you can read it* inside the cover, so if you're reading this the hope has been fulfilled, and the living and writing weren't in vain!

Ambling back to the beach at lunch-time I met a Dutchman washing clothes in a tub, and he lent it to me afterwards to do mine. He said he'd ridden his motocross bike down from Holland, and was on his way to Israel. I also washed my hair for the first time in over a week before strolling over to the other side of the peninsula; it was nice and quiet there, and I did some thinking while exploring new territory.

Sunday was quieter than a mouse's fart, and about as interesting, but on Monday the sun shone and we had our first work in Paleohora; Adam provided it, as he'd done the job before but found it too heavy with his bad back. We found out what he meant when we started the job, as it consisted of shovelling sand from the beach onto a pick-up, driving over to a half-built house, shovelling it back into buckets and carrying them up a couple of flights of stairs. We received 1,000 drachmas for three hours work, and afterwards returned to the beach and made peace with it; the swimming and sunbathing felt lush after the sweaty work. I was in a great mood, and although I knew bad times would return, I also thought they'd be followed by more good ones, in the never-ending cycle; well until death anyway, unless there's reincarnation.

K and I didn't get any more work that week, and lived a subsistence life. The highlight of the next day was chipping in with some of the other tent dwellers for pancakes, jam, baked potatoes, butter, wine and smoke. We ate and drank around a fire on the beach, although the nice atmosphere was tempered by dark clouds gathering above, while lightning flashes intermittently illuminated the distant ocean horizon.

I sent home pages of my diary and mementos like beer labels, coins and tickets on the Wednesday, meeting a bloke called Duncan I'd known in Chania at the post-office. He had good and bad news: the positive was that there was a party in a restaurant called Costello's later, while the negative was that the police had raided the beach community and told everyone to leave. Kenny knew about the raid when I saw him, but we didn't leave the beach. We frequented Vangeli's in the evening and drank grassi with the others, and then had trouble finding Costello's! Kenny got fed up with it and returned to the tent, but the rest of us found it soon after: there was English music playing, and free booze and food, although I gave the pig's trotters a miss! I talked with the Dutch biker and his girlfriend about Heavy Metal and Holland most of the time.

The Guns N' Roses Worker-Traveller

The wet weather and police hassle continued over the following days, and quite a few people left the village. This included Duncan, who'd arrived penniless and left the same way. Others arrived but didn't stay, like Gordon and Ally, who were to become significant to my story later. It meant there were more migrant workers in Paleohora than worker-travellers, and there were only three tents left on the beach until Harry put one up next to ours. He'd had to move out of his flat after a fight with his room-mate; a thirty year old German called Ray, who was the longest serving worker-traveller in Paleohora.

We also knew our days on the beach were numbered, and the need for new accommodation increased after heavy rain entered our tents and soaked the sleeping bags one night, and the next left puddles on the floor. The first night I slept with the wet sleeping-bag over me, but the tent was unusable on the second, so Kenny stayed with Harry and I slept in a half-built building. I awoke in the middle of the night with my socks still soaked and feet freezing, so I ran on the spot for a while to alleviate the latter!

We found a nice little cave that seemed the answer to our problem in the morning: you had to walk over some awkward rocks to gain access, but they also hid it from the village; and it was near the sea, but high enough that the water wouldn't reach. It had a low entrance you had to slide into, and there wasn't enough height inside to stand up in, but there was plenty of room for the three of us and our kit. It was a tonic after the wet tent and police hassle, and we made it more homely with polystyrene, beach mats, a quilt and blankets on the floor. We also had candles for night-time, and old pallets to use as firewood. There was a horseshoe-shaped space with the open end facing the sea between the cave-mouth and its sheltering rocks to cook. On the first evening we cooked up a veg stew feast and talked under a clear sky. Our new home, the food and grassi washing around inside us and the sparkling cosmos that provided our ceiling above inspired warm feelings and constant conversation.

The next morning was livened up by a high-spirited local driving onto the kerb of the café, while another grabbed a village simpleton and jokingly threatened to drive off. Adam was already on the cognac. I finished *Enemy Mine* and swapped it for *Last of the Mohicans* with Harry, who wasn't that impressed with the exchange. In the evening a drunken Ray accused Harry of nicking his stove, and H gave him a bloody nose with a hard slap.

Kenny got work with a builder called Magnioli on the Tuesday; Vangeli recommended him, and it was probably because K was skint and looked so bedraggled. I went inside after a while, having retired for the day, but then a farmer asked Vangeli for two workers and he nominated a Somalian and me. My work-mate spoke good English and we had a chat on the back of the pick-up as the farmer drove us into the mountains. Our job entailed ascending an olive grove and carrying scattered bags of olives down to the van. The combination of heavy bags and a lack of grip on my trainers caused me to fall over once as I descended the steep hill; although I was desperate for work I was quite glad there were only five bags each to carry! We were paid 500 drachmas each, and got a lift back to Paleohora. I started drinking with Kenny in the village, and the next day Harry said I was pissed when I returned to the cave: apparently I was rambling on about yellow penguins and looking for my sleeping bag while sitting on it!

The Guns N' Roses Worker-Traveller

I didn't work for the next three days as I was hung-over twice and there wasn't any on the other. After rising in mid-morning on the third I took our pots and cutlery over to the tap on the main beach to wash them. I was nearly finished when two policemen on a moped pulled up and asked me for my passport and details. I told them I didn't have my passport on me, didn't have much money, came from Britain and was sleeping on the beach. They left after one told me to leave town by noon the next day: *High Noon!* I later heard the police had also told other foreigners to leave, but I decided not to go, and thought they would forget about it.

The weekend was uneventful, but on Monday it was a gorgeous day, and after a couple of retsinas I went down the main beach with the others. Some went swimming, but I only had my old jeans with me so gave it a miss. However, I sunbathed topless for the first time in a long while, and it was a tonic to soak up the rays again. As the beach filled with sun-worshippers a football game broke out. I played in goal and defence, and did okay, but my lack of fitness showed when I played outfield; although the retsina probably didn't help either! I also tore a big hole down the crotch of my ragged jeans while stretching for the ball, which made them look even worse! The game lasted for an hour and was followed by more solar relaxation until sunset. Kenny, Adam and Vanessa went to a restaurant for a meal in the evening, but I didn't go as I hadn't worked and wasn't supposed to have any money; only Kenny knew I had traveller's cheques for future travel.

The next day was also warm and sunny, and in the morning Kenny worked with Magnioli. He'd also been offered a second job the previous night and passed it on to me, but by the time I arrived at the café

Marc Latham

Adam had already taken it! Harry also got work, and then returned to tell me of another job going, so I followed him over to a house being built on the edge of town. I grafted there with a middle-aged local who was good to work with; he even told me to slow down a few times as I tried to impress. I received 2,000 drachmas and lunch for the five hours of my time and toil, but there wasn't any more work. When I returned to the cave Kenny said he hadn't worked because the cement-mixer wouldn't start, while Harry said he only received 600 drachmas for three hours work.

I paid for our cave's supper that evening, and we cooked with Adam and Vanessa, who also brought food. The night started convivially, but after we'd finished the Spaghetti Bolognese and were getting stuck into the grassi Vanessa slapped Harry for some reason and he returned it. When the rest of us recovered from the shock we jumped between them and calmed the situation. In my drunken haze I later had a 1,000 drachma bet with Adam that I could see someone's head on the moonlit rocky horizon inland, as Kenny had gone to the village and I thought he might be returning. It was really foolish of me, as it was a grassi hallucination, and I lost the money. The others thought Adam shouldn't have kept the money, but I guess he was more desperate than me; he did have the look of an *Albert Steptoe* about him. Moreover, he was always suspecting travellers who passed through of having more money than they made out, so he probably thought I had more money than I displayed as well. He wasn't wrong, but to me the incident vindicated my decision not to tell them about my money. I also regretted telling them how much money I'd earned during the day, and suspected they didn't always tell the truth about their earnings.

The Guns N' Roses Worker-Traveller

I didn't get work the next two days, but in the morning of the second Vangeli gave me a pair of trousers; they weren't the height of fashion, but they fitted well and were a big improvement on the jeans. Like Kosta in Pirgos, the owner of the village work-café was a nice bloke, and his little act of kindness made my day. In the afternoon and evening we were joined by a Canadian called Richard and an Australian couple, Grant and Norma, who'd met elsewhere and travelled to Paleohora that day. They were just in town for a few days and were more like tourists than travellers. They became quite drunk in the evening, and while the men left to try out other bars, Norma stayed with us and came to a party after the café. There were about fifteen people there and most were Greek. The only music was from a lone guitar, but then that was curtailed by a broken string, and no replacement! However, there was plenty of grassi, so everybody soon forgot about the musical dilemma, and it was replaced by the sound of inebriated chatter. Norma got drunk as the night progressed, and was having trouble keeping some of the men off her, so I walked her home after a couple of hours. She'd seemed fascinated by our hobo lifestyles and said she'd love to see our cave, so I thought I could probably get off with her, but just walked her home before returning to our grotto. K and H were pissed when they returned, and jokingly refused to believe nothing had happened with Norma.

H slept in the next morning, while K and I tried for work. K was still drunk from the previous night, and after giving up on work he decided to return to Pirgos; he thought some money had been sent to him there, and said that he was going to look for work on the way. After collecting his rucksack from the cave he shared a retsina with me before we exchanged addresses and bade farewell. He said he'd phone on Monday evening if he found work. I had mixed feelings about his departure, as he still owed me 3,000 drachmas and we'd had a few quarrels, but he'd also done me a few favours and had generally been okay.

After he left I sat with H and some of his Greek friends: Rui, Ellis and Stelios. Just before lunchtime a lorry passed the café loaded with machinery, and Vangeli suggested we ask the driver if he needed help. So we followed it to the olive factory and the driver hired us to guide the machinery he was unloading by crane; there wasn't any lifting so it wasn't hard work, and we were *over the moon* to receive 2,000 drachmas each for three hours. We went to Ellis's room for a wash after finishing, and followed that with a nice restaurant meal and a game of kaluki for a beer; Harry and I beat Rui and Ellis. R and E had travelled down from the north of Greece together, and said there was often animosity between Cretans and mainland Greeks, as many of the former didn't consider themselves as Greek. We ended up in the only disco remaining open over the winter; there were just a few worker-travellers there and the beer was expensive, but they played some good tunes and I enjoyed being in that kind of atmosphere again.

I didn't get work the next morning and passed the time with Vanessa, learning some Greek words and how to make cotton bracelets. It was a sunny day and I later frequented the beach to eat lunch, read *Mohicans* and have a walk. I was quite enjoying the post-Kenny age, but when I returned to Vangeli's in the afternoon he'd returned! He said he'd walked for ages on the path towards Pirgos but had only seen a couple of cars and didn't get a lift. He'd lain out in the cold overnight and didn't get much sleep, so headed back in the morning.

I didn't bother looking for work in the morning. It

was Sunday, and Harry was leaving for another village the day after, so we cooked round a fire near our cave in the afternoon along with his Greek friends. We had sausages, baked potatoes, Greek salad and bread, washed down with grassi and retsina. Harry also invited Kenny, but he went off with Adam and Vanessa instead. It was a good meal with nice company on a warm sunny day, and it was events like that, combined with laziness and optimism, that kept me in Paleohora. We continued the party in Ellis's room after dark, but I couldn't remember much there.

I awoke on a bed in another room when somebody was leaving, but I didn't know where I was or how I'd arrived, and there was no sign of my jacket and day-bag. I felt awful and had the shits, so I stayed there until late afternoon. I frequented Vangeli's after leaving and Ray filled me in on the previous night's events: apparently I was asleep for most of the party and he carried me to his flat when it finished. I was relieved nothing bad had happened, and after returning to Ellis's I also found my jacket, but my day-bag was still missing. I visited Adam's new cave with Kenny in the evening. Adam was now on his own after Vanessa left with Harry in the morning; I'd always thought Adam and Vanessa were together, but apparently they were just friends. We ate stew and they caned wine, but I didn't drink.

I awoke after light entered the cave in the morning; Harry had taken his alarm clock so we had no way of telling the time anymore. I looked for my bag near the cave again, and was relieved to find it; especially as it was in a place I wouldn't have dreamt of leaving it if I was sober!

The good start to the day continued after reaching Vangeli's, as Rui said he might have work for me unloading beer wagons. He bought me a coffee, and the lorries arrived soon after. Apart from me there were four Greeks supposed to work. However, Ray then turned up and accused Rui of nicking his job. He made such a fuss Yanni left, and Ray took his place. After all that fuss the work soon proved too heavy for Ray, and he jacked it in after an hour. The rest of us unloaded crates of beer and then loaded the trucks up with empties, which took four hours; we could drink beer as we worked, and I had a few. The four of us who finished the job got 3,500 drachmas each and paid for Yanni's meal at a restaurant, as he'd done some work but hadn't received any money. Then we went to Rui's flat for a wash, and my dopiness showed up again, as I had an all-over wash in the sink before noticing the shower Rui had meant me to use! Anyway, I was basically clean for the first time in ages, was well-fed, had some money and my bag, and so was on a bit of a high. I hoped the good luck would continue, but should have known that after a high there is usually a low around the corner!

The next morning didn't start well, as there was no work, but then it got much worse. Three policemen arrived to check passports, and they included the one who'd told me to leave town. I didn't think he'd remember me, and tried not to look at him, but it was to no avail, as he recognised me straight away! He looked at me with hatred in his eyes, and after a short questioning took my passport and told me I could collect it before leaving town. They also took the other foreigners' passports, but Kenny told them he didn't have one and they took him with them. The experienced campaigner, Adam, hid in the toilets the whole time.

So after spending weeks deliberating about whether to leave Paleohora the decision was made for

The Guns N' Roses Worker-Traveller

me, and after recovering from the shock I was quite relieved. I returned to the cave and packed, before spending an hour reminiscing on the main beach. Paleohora was beautiful, and we'd had some good times, but it'd also been a struggle! Then I went over the station and collected my passport with a swagger the policeman who'd remembered me obviously didn't like; he looked disappointed I'd collected it, and I was to find out why later. Back over Vangeli's I said farewell to the others. Kenny said they'd put him in a cell for a while and told him to leave town, but he didn't have enough money. I could've lent him the dosh, but he still owed me thousands, and to tell you the truth I was as glad to be escaping him as Paleohora. Then the *high noon* bus arrived, and I enthusiastically boarded it; Ellis and Yanni were also on the bus, but I only bought a ticket to the next village.

After disembarking I ordered a coke in the only café in town, and asked about work with the Greek words Vanessa taught me; I said *Ekkis duila akee* or something, but the woman looked at me comically, and didn't seem to know what I was on about! So after downing the cola I started hitching north, and an interesting afternoon ensued: I had a couple of lifts in the back of pick-ups, with walks in the mountains in between, and ate a lunch of bread I bought and oranges picked from a tree. I also asked about work in another couple of villages with my pidgin Greek, but again had negative responses. I wasn't that bothered, and felt euphoric revelling in the freedom of the sun-kissed mountains, motioning hello to people we passed, with Bon Jovi's *Wanted Dead or Alive* rotating in my head.

I'd been walking for a while as it darkened, so I was mentally preparing myself for a night under the stars, but then a car picked me up and took me into

Marc Latham

Chania. I also saw several worker-travellers milling about in a few villages on the way, and thought I'd give them a go if Chania hadn't improved. I headed to the Green Bar after getting dropped off, and while drinking a beer and writing my diary a woman commented on my small writing, so I got talking to her. She spoke English fluently with a Brummie accent but said she was Norwegian, and her name was Cassie. She was living in Platanias, one of the nearby villages, and said the work situation was good there. Nobby, Ellis and Yanni were also in the bar, and said hello. After leaving to look for somewhere to sleep I got side-tracked by Heavy Metal coming out of a bar called Club 61; I only intended listening to a couple of tracks but ended up spending over an hour outside there. After getting my fill of Metal I bedded down alongside a hotel on the edge of town. I was glad to be out of Paleohora, but missed some of the people, the beach and cave.

I frequented the Green Bar in the morning, but didn't get a sniff of work. However, I met Dom, a French-Canadian bloke that had lived on the beach in Paleohora. We talked for ages before he left for the nearby village of Vrises. In the afternoon I left my rucksack in the Green Bar and walked round town. I saw new albums by Kiss (Crazy Nights) and WASP (Live...In the Raw) in a shop, and ate bread and feta cheese. I enjoyed the stroll, but having had my fix of civilisation, and with no work or accommodation on the horizon, I decided to leave Chania for the villages I'd passed on the way. After collecting my rucksack and seeing a fight between a drunk and a waiter across at Costa's I walked to the edge of town and stuck my thumb out.

I got a lift almost immediately to a village called Agia Marina, but didn't have any luck hitching from

The Guns N' Roses Worker-Traveller

there. So I started walking and soon came across a sign stating that Platanias was half a mile away; it was the village Cassie had recommended the previous night, so I thought I'd give it a try. After arriving in the village I frequented a café containing several worker-travellers, and joined Cassie and a thirty year old Scot called Donald; they were drinking cognacs and were really friendly. We were then joined by other people returning from work: an Englishman called Bernie, who was my age and had been travelling in Europe since May, and Ally and Gordon, both of whom I'd briefly met in Paleohora. Ally was my age and Scottish, while Gordon was a little older and Australian.

The café became busy after a while, and I later met Ally's mate Joe, a Welsh bloke called Dai, who was forty-ish, and just down for the night as he had a regular job in the mountains; and another forty-something called Jamie, who had started travelling on ships and never kicked the habit. We had a good laugh, with Dai's life story the main topic, although I was warned he was a bit of a bullshitter. At the end of the night I was going to doss down on the beach, but the Scots said they'd put me up in their room.

So I followed them on the road leading west out of town for about fifteen minutes, until we came to a garden path leading inland to a big white house. They unlocked their room, one of two now rented out by the family who also lived in the house, and welcomed me inside. There were two beds, a cupboard, stove and sink inside, and an adjacent bathroom. They gave me a mat to put under my sleeping bag and I slept on the floor. I seemed to have landed on my feet, and was happy that I'd found great company and had a roof over my head.

I went over to the work-café with the Scots in the morning, but rain limited employment possibilities. Joe and Jamie had a regular job, but even they didn't work. So I took the bus into Chania with Gordon, Ally and Joe in the late morning, and after a meal we frequented Costa's; needless to say I felt a sense of déjà vu! I met Dom again there, and he said he was starting a job in the Vrises olive factory on Sunday. While I talked to him a Danish bloke who'd also been in Paleohora joined us, and said that on the night of my departure Kenny and a couple of others who'd stayed were dragged out of Vangeli's by the police and beaten up. I was sorry to hear it, but also felt Kenny's was karma-ish, as he hadn't helped me much in Pirgos or made much effort to pay the money he owed me back. It was the last I ever heard of Kenny, so I don't know what happened to him afterwards.

There was heavy rain all night and into the next morning so there was no work again the next day. When the precipitation eased I walked over to the next village with Ally and Gordon, and met my cave-dwelling mate, Harry, in their work-café. He said a local had threatened him and his friend with a shotgun the previous night, and they'd had to make a hasty exit. Before we left he gave me an old pair of work-boots he was throwing away, as there was a hole in the left one, and he'd just bought a pair of wellies. They weren't ideal, but they were a big improvement on my raggedy trainers.

I was one of two left without work in the café the next morning after the early rush, along with another British bloke called Paul. Then a Greek worker-traveller called Toka came over and said he needed someone to work alongside him in the mountains, and it paid 2,500 drachmas a day plus food and accommodation. It was

The Guns N' Roses Worker-Traveller

the kind of job most people wanted, and we were no different, so we tossed a coin; Paul called but got it wrong, so I got the job. I felt really lucky, as I thought winning the toss would net me hundreds of pounds, but in the end it didn't turn out to be worth much.

Toka and I left straight away with the farmer who'd employed us so I just took my day-bag with me, as I couldn't get my rucksack out of Ally and Joe's because they were away working. We travelled high into the mountains, and soon after arriving at the farm Toka and I started picking oranges along with the boss's elderly parents. After a couple of hours we stopped for a lunch of meat, potatoes in olive oil, bread and grassi, and then continued picking until 3 p.m., when we started carrying crates of oranges out of the field. The latter was the hardest work of the day; at first we took them straight out to a tractor, which wasn't too bad, but then we had to carry them up a steep hill, which was tough. We'd filled 130 crates, and moved all but twenty before finishing.

We were then taken to the parents' house, where we were to lodge, as the boss lived in Chania. After the boss left we realised he'd taken our bags, and this was a bad blow to me as my asthma inhaler was inside and I'd started to wheeze towards the end of work, probably brought on by a cold I'd had for a few days. We had chips, bread and feta for supper, and then Toka and I went down to the only café in the village for a few beers. There were quite a few locals inside, and some were drunkenly playing pranks on each other, such as lighting newspapers and putting them under each others' seats. A Charles Bronson film and *MacGyver* were on television, but I couldn't really follow them because they used subtitles and kept the volume low.

After returning to the house I slept okay, but was desperate for the toilet in the morning and didn't know where it was. So I went into an olive grove behind the house and had a #2 there, using old cement bag paper to wipe afterwards. Toka had risen by the time I returned, and we had bread and feta for breakfast, with a tea made from wild leaves to drink. At work we had a similar day to the previous, but at lunch-time I gave most of my meat to Toka, as there was loads of fat on it. The boss returned my day-bag in the afternoon and I was relieved to have a blow on the inhaler, although it didn't totally relieve my wheezing. After work we got dropped off at the café and had a couple of coffees and a chat. Toka had spent three years working on ships, visiting Australia and the US amongst other places, so he spoke good English. He said he was twenty-three and from northern Greece, although he'd been living in Athens before Crete. We also discussed our current job, and he informed me we were to pick olives after oranges and work until January, with just a day off for Christmas; however, everything changed the next day, and I was back in Platanias by the end of it!

The mother's shouting woke us in the morning, as we'd slept in. We had a quick breakfast before work, but were still late starting. The grove had a serene beauty about it when we arrived: the post-dawn sun lit up dew covered trees for the eyes, the water falling from leaves and oranges provided a cooling sensation for the body, while the silence of the mountains was golden for the mind. However, the day went downhill after that. Firstly, I'd left my jacket somewhere the day before and couldn't find it, then Toka really *upset my applecart* in the orange grove when he said he was returning to Athens because of a blister on his foot. I continued working until the end of the day, but after Toka informed the boss of his decision I was told they weren't going to

The Guns N' Roses Worker-Traveller

work for a few days and I wasn't needed. The gaffer said he'd come and collect me when they started again, but I didn't hold out much hope for that. He paid me 5,000 drachmas for the work I'd done and gave me a lift to Platanias, before taking Toka to Chania.

Ally, Gordon, Joe, Jamie and a few others were in the work-café when I got there. I had a good welcome and they'd all had plenty of work, so any regret I had about losing the mountain job soon disappeared. I was buzzing from my homecoming, so after a few beers I went onto retsina, and I'm sure you don't need me to tell you what happened next!

The next thing I remember was coming to my senses down on the beach near some worker-traveller tents. I was wearing a denim jacket with a woollen inner I didn't remember acquiring, and nobody ever claimed. Then I made my way back to the village, which was a bit of a mission in itself. After making it to Ally and Joe's room I tried to sleep outside for a while as it was late, but it proved to be too cold and uncomfortable, so I knocked on the door and Ally let me in.

I woke when the other two left in the morning, but I was still hung-over and didn't rise. However, Ally then returned and said he had work for me, so I dragged myself up from the floor and reluctantly went off to graft. The farmer drove us out to an olive grove, and our job was to climb trees and beat olives onto a big mat on the ground. I felt nauseous from the hangover and was praying for rain to fall from the cloudy sky. Moreover, my wrist injury meant I couldn't use my right hand to hit the olives, and my left wasn't very co-ordinated! However, although the work was quite excruciating we had a good laugh during the day, as the farmer reminded Ally of Skippy the bush kangaroo off the TV, and he was going on about it all the time. The rain finally fell in the late morning, and I showed some enthusiasm for the first time that day as I jumped down and raced to the car. We had lunch with a view to returning to work, but the downpour thankfully worsened and Skippy drove us home.

Most of the others had also been rained off, and we had a good afternoon in the work-café, chatting and watching Greece lose 3-0 at home to Holland in a European qualifier. In the evening I started renting a flat with Gordon for 400 drachmas a night each, as there seemed to be enough work and I didn't want to outstay my welcome with the Scots. It was next door to their flat, and had the same layout. It was my first room away from home, so it was quite exciting. I looked forward to sleeping in my bed but was disappointed when it happened, as I felt cold despite being in my sleeping bag with the blanket over me.

I devoured a cheese pie on the way to the work-café in the morning, and it was so cheap and delicious it became my default breakfast. Ally and I were supposed to work with Skippy again, and turned down a few jobs before he finally turned up. He had a couple of women with him that seemed to be his wife and sister. One of the women was a bit of a tyrant, and shouted at us regularly through the day. We weren't bothered though, and just gave it back. She tripped over the mat at one stage, which was the highlight of the day for us; we laughed so hard we nearly toppled out of the tree! We had a hearty lunch and got paid 2,500 drachmas, but the tyrant told Ally she didn't want me to work for them again. It didn't bother me, as there was loads of other work around anyway.

Back in Platanias we had a beer with the others

and shared our news, before I bought a pair of wellies and some razors. After cooking and eating with Ally I had my first shower since Rome three months before, although I didn't get under fully as the water was cold. I also shaved for the first time in two months after cutting the whiskers off with a scissors; the mountain man looked civilised! It was cold again in bed, so I decided to wear clothes inside my sleeping-bag from then on.

It rained all night and looked like it might start again in the morning, but I worked all day picking oranges. The oranges suited me much better than the olives because of my dodgy wrist, so I was always glad to get that work. A couple Gordon knew gave us and Ally a lift into Chania in the evening. The couple were nice old hippies called Neville and Anne, and we had a cool drive in the back of their funky transit with music blaring out of the sound system. After arriving in Chania they went to meet friends, while we frequented Costa's. We met Donald and Joe there; they'd been drinking in Chania all day, and Joe said he'd just had a fight. While we were there I was offered a regular job starting in the morning, but it was too late now! Gordon, Ally and I went to the cinema to watch *Lethal Weapon* at 10 p.m.. I lost the others for half the film, as I went to the toilet before the lights dimmed and couldn't find them afterwards! The film was okay, but it was difficult to follow as they used Greek subtitles and had the sound turned down. After the film we descended into The Labyrinth (disco-bar) and met up with Joe and Donald again. There weren't many people inside, but there was some good sixties and seventies music playing.

After arriving home we went to our separate rooms, but then Gordon and I heard a racket from next door. By the time we got outside to see what was going on the two Scots were fighting with each other in the garden, with Joe on the offensive. Ally was strong but small, and Joe was a big powerful bloke. After we stopped the fight Joe went inside their room and locked Ally out, so the wee Scot came over to ours, but just as we'd begun to regain our composure Joe reappeared and tried to grab Ally. Gordon was standing near them and stopped Joe long enough for Ally to make his escape through the window, as Joe was blocking the door. Gordon then did a good job of cooling Joe down, but after he returned to their room Ally soon reappeared in ours, and we locked the door before going to bed. It had been a hectic night, but a good one!

I had only been in the work-café for a few minutes the next morning when Bernie asked me to work in the olive factory. I jumped at the chance, and we spent a sunny morning being driven into the mountains to collect sacked olives. Most of the time was spent travelling, which suited Bernie and me, as we didn't do as much work and spent more time viewing the impressive scenery: olive groves interlaced with pine forests where we worked, and panoramic views of the blue and gold coast below. The olive sacks were quite heavy, but not too bad between the two of us, as Bernie was a strong lad. We had a two hour lunch-break, so I went over the work-café and talked with Joe and Ally, who'd made up after the previous night. They'd worked with Skippy for an hour but couldn't take the verbal, so they'd jacked it in. Bernie and I had a similar afternoon to the morning, and at the end of the day received 3,000 drachmas. We were also told we had regular work if we wanted it. I bought Bernie a beer after returning to the café, before eating at home with Ally and Gordon. I updated my diary afterwards, as I'd gone five days without doing it; the longest time since leaving home. The others went into Chania for a big Saturday night, but I didn't go as I had work in the morning.

The Guns N' Roses Worker-Traveller

I worked with a German called Tom first thing the next morning, but when Bernie arrived an hour later I collected olives with him and the boss until finishing at lunch-time. Bernie had been in Chania the previous night and said they'd had a good time, but got chucked out of Costa's and the Green Bar in the process! After returning to the café we were told we'd just missed a fight between Dai and Donald, with Dai apparently going for him out of nowhere. Joe and Jamie were leaving for a job in the mountains, so we had a few beers and a laugh before saying goodbye to them.

I had 25,000 drachmas, a steady job, a room and some good friends, so I felt great about life in Platanias, and was looking forward to Christmas. It was so different to Paleohora, where there was no work and everybody was poncing off each other; just a couple of hours away, but like another world!

I worked in the olive factory for the next three days, and finished for Christmas on Wednesday the 23rd at 4 p.m.. I'd worked inside the factory most of the time, while Bernie was still going up collecting sacks. I missed the trips into the mountains, but it had also been quite wet, so I was happy to be under cover when it rained. I also felt fortunate to have the factory job, as there wasn't much picking work going on because of the rain, and some of the others were struggling for money. Joe and Jamie also returned early from the mountains, as they'd been treated badly.

There was a vibrant atmosphere inside the café in the evening that immediately warmed my heart and put a smile on my face. Some of the regulars were there, as well as a few new faces that had either just arrived in the village or returned from the mountains for Christmas: the new additions included a funny

Marc Latham

Australian called Manny, a big South African called Ted, a mellow Irish bloke called Connor, an easy going dude from Birmingham called Hector, and a couple of lads from Newport and Chepstow that went by the names of Stan and Claude. I was in a great mood all night, and kept up my tradition of celebrating the start of the Christmas holiday in style with six or seven bottles of retsina. I lost my memory by the end, but behaved okay by all accounts.

Manny slept on our floor as he was homeless and I woke briefly the next morning when the others went to work. I rose later, and after breakfast updated my diary in preparation for neglecting it over the next few days, as I planned a good holiday. Around midday I boarded the bus to Chania with an agenda all set out, but my plans *went down the pan* after Bernie and Ted also boarded. I spent the day with them, and we went to the usual bars after eating. They played the Scorpions' *Worldwide Live* in Costa's, which made me recollect home; I wondered if my old mates were also out *on the piss* in town. Like a time-travelling messenger from those days Ted then told me he'd bought some Ponderal, and explained they were slimming pills which gave you an amphetamine effect; so when we passed the next chemist I bought 100 for 850 drachmas, with ten supposed to be enough for a good effect. We also visited the house of somebody they thought might have dope, but they didn't have any, and we just drank grassi with them instead. I took my first ten pills in Costa's after meeting up with Cassie, Hector and another couple, and we later returned to Platanias together in two taxis.

When we arrived back and walked in the café the atmosphere, alcohol and tablets blew my mind, as everyone was partying after all the hardship and boredom we'd endured. Donald led the singing and some people were juggling, while the rest of us just got wasted. I took another ten pills soon after returning, and gave twenty to Cassie and Ted; I only had fifty left the next day so probably took another ten later. I couldn't remember that much about the night, but was told I was getting on well with an American girl before falling into a stupor. They said they got worried about me at one stage, as I wasn't responding to them at all.

    The Scots woke Gordon and me on Christmas Day at around midday, and the four of us got a taxi into Chania to look for dinner. It was a bit of a mission, as most places were closed, but we eventually found a restaurant open and had a basic meal and a beer for 750 drachmas each. They had MTV on their television and we watched that for a while before getting a taxi back to Platanias. Joe and Gordon felt ill and went home, but Ally and I frequented the work-café; after taking another ten pills I was ready for another big night! Donald, Connor, Jamie and a few of the others had been drinking all day, and the café had run out of beer and wine, so we were allowed to bring it in from the supermarket. There was almost a fight soon after we arrived: a local gave a singing worker-traveller money as if paying a beggar, and the worker threw it away, which angered the local. Jamie later fell off his chair and was funny throughout the night, repetitively telling us he was a hopeless alcoholic. Ally also got paralytic by the end of the night and I walked him home, as I was quite sober after the pills. The café was still out of beer and wine the next day, so we relocated to the Hotel Platanias and Yanni's in the evening. I took ten pills again, and was then drinking three beers to the others' one without getting drunk, so I went on the retsina and that did the trick! I lost my memory after a while, and was later told Connor carried me home after I fell over a couple of times, and that I was singing *California Girls* and *Surfing USA* back in the flat.

I rose to watch the traditional local derby between Platanias and Chania the next afternoon. It was played on a pitch close to the beach in Platanias and cost 200 drachmas to watch. A fine day, the nicest for a while, meant there was a bumper crowd that must have been in the hundreds. The match ended all square at 1-1, and everybody seemed satisfied with that. I headed into Chania after the game, with buying more Ponderal the main objective; however, I couldn't find an open chemist when I got there, and in the end bought a jumper from the market for 1,500 drachmas instead. After food I watched *Full Metal Jacket*, as I'd intended doing on Christmas Eve. I enjoyed the film but didn't think it was as good as *Platoon*. After returning to Platanias I took another ten pills and had a good night with the usual crowd. An Englishman, Barry, and a Scottish lass called Gwash arrived in the village and joined in with us. After returning to the room I couldn't sleep for most of the night because of the pills, and heard a drunken Manny sleepwalk into Gordon's table during the night. He was still out of it as Gordon guided him back to his sleeping-bag on the floor.

I returned to work the next day; the olive factory was closed, so I went on a job with Manny and Ally. The farmer was only paying us 2,000 drachmas each for the day so we took it easy. I struggled because it was olive-beating, so they thought I was lazy. We worked topless most of the time as it was another nice day and the sun got quite hot, although we could see the snow-capped White Mountains living up to their name in the distance.

Ally and Manny worked for him again the next

The Guns N' Roses Worker-Traveller

day but they didn't want me, so Gordon went instead. I wasn't bothered anyway, as they didn't pay much and it was a warm sunny day; I also hoped to get a better paid job, but nothing materialised. In the late morning I visited the next village with Donald and Gwash. We walked along the beach until the river cut us off, and then had to wade through thick vegetation to get to the road. After arriving in the village we drank a beer in their work-café and I talked to Yanni from Paleohora, who was living and working there now. It was really quiet there, and it wasn't long before we returned to Platanias. We were joined outside our work-café by Hector, Connor, Cassie and a few others. Donald had talked about his ex-fiancée to me for the first time on the walk, and then she turned up on a moped!

After returning to my room I did my good deed for the day by carrying some olive sacks into the house for the grandmother...and not even charging her! When Ally returned from work he said they'd asked the boss for more money but he turned them down flat, so they weren't going to work for him again. Manny later moved out of our room and into the Hotel Platanias, as Gordon said the grandmother had earlier said she knew there were more than two people staying in the room.

I worked over the olive factory for the next couple of days with a portly little local called Jorgo; his face was full of life and character, but he seemed quite ill with a cough. The second day was New Year's Eve, but I started work as normal. After an enjoyable morning I had a bottle of retsina with the others at lunchtime, but as the alcohol wore off and I was keen to get the evening under way the afternoon dragged. It might also have had something to do with the pills I'd previously taken, as I was depressed and angry when I should have been in a good mood. I eventually finished at 6, and my mood brightened when I met Gordon and Ally at the house, as they hadn't long finished work either, but deflated when Gordon said the shower wouldn't be hot for a while as he'd just used it. I couldn't wait to start partying, so just got it over with and had a cold one! Then I excitedly dressed in my best clothes, took twenty pills, and made my way over the café. Ted gave me another ten pills soon after I arrived, so I was flying! Some of the others got the bus to Chania at 8, but I waited for a lift in the funky transit along with Ted, Gordon and Manny.

We had a great laugh singing and joking on the journey, and my afternoon stress was long forgotten. We frequented Costa's upon arrival, and were met by a zombified Barry sitting outside talking to himself; he'd also been on the pills! Costa's was followed by Scorpio's, and everybody started getting into the party spirit there. I'd bought some canvas shoes for the night but took them off as they were uncomfortable for dancing and then lost them, so I walked round in socks for the rest of the time! We ended up in The Labyrinth, which was totally anarchic, with a cocktail of scruffy drunks, alcohol and mud swirling around on the dark, cavernous dance-floor. There were few women there. Ally and Joe had a few fights with other people during the night, while I just had a couple of brief scuffles; I was relieved to have avoided most of it. I danced and drank, losing my mind somewhere along the way. The first time I remember noticing it was 1988 was about 3 or 4 a.m..

Harry turned up early the next afternoon and asked if we wanted to play football. I don't know what sparked the idea, but we had the sense to turn him down flat! A couple of hours later Ally returned from Chania still looking pissed. He also had blood over his clothes and his knuckles were shredded. Most of us got

The Guns N' Roses Worker-Traveller

pissed again in the work-café during the night, and Joe had another fight.

I didn't intend working the next day either, but saw Jorgo in the morning, and he persuaded me to work in the factory. There was no work there the next day and I didn't look for anything else. Gordon left for northern Europe in the morning, so I underwent the goodbye ritual with my first flatmate; we'd got on well, and he said I'd behaved better than he'd expected. I later frequented the work-café, where Barry gave me a listen to Dave Lee Roth's new *Eat 'em and Smile* album on his walkman; it was cool. I also played backgammon with him and Manny for 500 drachmas a game. We ended up all square after I drew 1-1 with Manny and lost a double or quits with Barry after winning the first two. I had an early night as I was working in the factory the next morning, but the village had quietened down after the holiday celebrations anyway, and many of those who'd shared the good times had now left.

I'd had some problems with my chest over the previous few days, probably brought on by the combination of drab weather and partying excess, but it had been under control until rapidly deteriorating one afternoon in the olive factory. It was a shocking experience having severe asthma again, and especially being away from home and the security of a medical service you have knowledge of. I'd had to have home visits by doctors a few times as a child, and injections to alleviate my condition; one of which gave me my first remembered high, after I was too shy to tell the doctor a first injection had affected me, and he gave me a second! I felt like I could have done with an injection in the factory, but instead struggled back to my room for puffs on an inhaler during a break. However, they didn't alleviate the problem, and my chest remained tight. I had to breathe more deeply and rapidly as less air reached my lungs, and as I walked back to the factory feeling uncomfortable and weak I knew I was in for a horrible few hours. Some of the others noticed I was having difficulty after I returned to the factory but I continued grafting despite my situation worsening. Bernie left at six as he'd arranged, but work continued and didn't look like ending, so at seven I said I had to finish, as I could hardly breathe; just my luck we had our longest day when I had terrible asthma!

After leaving work I stopped to try and breathe deeply a few times along the short walk to my room, which enabled me to make it home, but didn't improve matters much. I was relieved to get home without any of my friends seeing me, as I wouldn't have been able to talk properly. After reaching the flat I took one of the asthma antibiotics I had for emergencies and sat in the bathroom, as I was embarrassed by my breathless state and didn't want the others to see me if they called around. I had a shower after the water heated up, and as the antibiotic took effect I felt comfortable enough to relocate to the bedroom afterwards. However, I still had to sit rigid on the edge of the bed, as the effort needed to breathe meant I couldn't relax.

My fears about being seen by the others were realised when Joe and Jamie called around. They seemed shocked at my state, as I could only talk in short bursts between trying to breathe deeply. They suggested I return to the UK, but I said it would soon pass. Ally also came over to see how I was later; it was nice of them to show concern but I felt like a freak, and thought the weakness and vulnerability I displayed undermined the rock n' roll wild man image I tried to present to my public! After they left I took another antibiotic and more of the inhaler, read *Mohicans* and got to sleep, but woke three or four times in the night and took the inhaler again each time. There were a couple of other such attacks on my travels, brought on by partying excess, damp conditions or extreme temperature fluctuations, but I knew it was a risk I had to live with if I wanted to see the world.

I was much better by mid morning the next day and, although not breathing normally, could relax while sitting, and walk around comfortably. Mirroring the calm after the storm in my body it was a beautiful day outside, and I joined in with a football game between locals and worker-travellers on a gravel pitch; it was seven-a-side, but I only knew Hector and Manny on our team, as the others were working. We played for about an hour and I did okay considering the asthma. I tried to conserve my energy as much as possible, playing in the sweeper role as it meant I only had to run when they attacked.

I spent the rest of the day down on the beach and in the café, until returning to the room and eating with the two Scots. They were glad to see my health had improved. The next morning was also sunny, and after failing to get employed I went over to the pier with Ally and Manny. Ally tried fishing with some wire he found but soon lost patience with it after nothing bit. We bussed into Chania in the afternoon and watched *Hamburger Hill*, which I thought was better than *Full Metal Jacket*, but not as good as *Platoon*. My asthma seemed to loosen up in the cinema and I coughed up copious amounts of multicoloured phlegm afterwards.

As my health had improved I looked for work at the olive factory the next morning, but the boss said there was no work for me. I didn't know if it was because I'd been ill, or left when there was still work to do, but he didn't seem too happy with me, as Bernie got work later.

I sat with Ally and Claude at the work-café until they got work with Skippy, but Ally returned soon after saying he'd had enough and walked! Ally got more work in the afternoon, while I bought my first bar of soap since leaving home; a soap-dodger no more! I had no luck when I tried the olive factory again the next morning, although the boss said I should try again on Monday. I returned to the café and sat with Ally and Stan until they got work picking oranges along with several others. There were a lot of migrant workers in the village now, and it was getting harder to find work.

All my Platanias friends were now working and I was thinking of going back to the flat until Harry arrived with an Israeli friend called Ussi. A couple of blokes from Derby, Walter and Zebedy, and a Danish guy, Lars, also arrived in Platanias and were a laugh; they'd been on a kibbutz together and were over for a holiday. I didn't know it at the time, but I would soon be sailing away from Crete with four of the five people with whom I was unexpectedly spending my day.

I later put my work woes behind me with a Saturday night out in Chania. After a few retsinas in Platanias we had another lift in the funky transit, with Donald, Ted and Joe particularly vocal. Most of the others went for a meal after arriving, but Donald and I frequented Scorpio's before meeting up with them in The Labyrinth. I got drunk and lost my memory after a while, and the next I remembered was waking up at home early the next afternoon. I frequented the café in the evening and Donald told me I'd wanted to walk back to Chania after they'd brought me back to Platanias in a taxi!

Bad weather and no luck at the olive factory meant I didn't work for the first two days of the week. I

The Guns N' Roses Worker-Traveller

was down to 8,000 drachmas, had no work on the horizon and felt bored. Together with the desire for new horizons, my Platanias plight made me decide to leave for Israel the next day. When I told Ally my news he was pissed-off, as he was also feeling down and wanted to leave. We later visited Bernie, who was in bed with flu. He said he was thinking of going home because of his illness and generally feeling down, so we fetched Stan from the café, as he was trying to sell a return ticket to England.

After we'd returned to the work-café and Ally had gone home for lunch a farmer arrived looking for a couple of workers, so Stan and I obliged. We had an easy three hours picking oranges off low branches and filled eighty crates. We got paid 1,100 drachmas each, and I thought it was a fitting finale to my career on Crete, after about three months working in three villages and a town. We didn't get a lift back, but that wasn't a problem, and I enjoyed the hike knowing new horizons beckoned the next day. We celebrated Jamie's forty-fourth birthday and my leaving during the night; it was a good laugh, with a paralytic Jamie dancing around to music the highlight. I bought Jamie a beer, and others bought me one; including Bernie, who'd given Donald the money from his sick-bed. Ally'd got a regular building-site job off Hector, so he was in a better mood. After returning to the room I paid the rent up to date and got my passport. Donald slept in the spare bed as he was homeless.

Ally called over in the morning and woke Donald for work, and I said goodbye to both of them as they left. I dozed for a while before rising, and then washed, packed and left my first room. As I closed the door for the last time I thought about the good and bad memories, with the camaraderie and drunken laughs the main positive ones, and the asthma and arguments the negative. I walked over to the village, eating my final Cretan cheese pie on the way, and sat outside the work-café for the last time. The Chania bus came at 10:30, and I left a Cretan village under good circumstances for the first time: third time lucky! I bade farewell to Connor and Stan, and asked them to say goodbye to the others. When I boarded the bus it sunk in that I was off on my own again, to new countries for the first time in months, which was both exciting and invigorating.

I took some clothes to the launderette after reaching Chania, before going to the harbour for some thinking time: *sitting on the dock of the bay II*! As I walked back towards town I met Walter, Lars and Zebedy, and they were also sailing for Athens that day, on their way back to Israel. So we visited the port and bought tickets to Athens; mine cost 2,000 drachmas, while Walter's only cost 1,100 with a dodgy student card, so I put a card on the top of my shopping list! We met Ussi at the port and he was sailing on the same boat as us, so we boarded together and were pleasantly surprised to find we had a bed each in shared cabins.

We set sail at 7 p.m., and as land disappeared from view I knew I'd finally escaped Crete. I wasn't sorry to have left, but thinking about the previous three months I also remembered some great times as well; Galini seemed a long time ago, and life had been pretty rough after the idyllic start, but fun and laughs were never absent for long.

The five of us played cards after eating and it was another good time, with plenty of banter from the three returning to the kibbutz. It was very different to my solitary journey over to Crete. We later watched a couple of films: *Brewster's Millions* and *Five Desperate*

The Guns N' Roses Worker-Traveller

Women, before bedding down. As I lay my head on the pillow I knew I wouldn't be waking on Crete the next morning; something I'd often dreamt about while on the island.

I woke as we arrived in Piraeus, twelve hours after leaving Chania. It was still dark, so we got a coffee in a harbour café and sat outside. While there, Barry from Platanias arrived out of nowhere and said he was working as a painter for the Hilton hotel! If another had joined us it would have resembled the assembling of the *Magnificent Seven*, but we remained a Shady Six, and our mission to buy a boat ticket didn't quite compare with saving a Mexican village! After checking Haifa ticket prices in the port shops we walked into Athens to enquire there. I bought a cheese pie and a *Daily Mirror* on the way. The ticket prices seemed as expensive in the city as in the port, so we returned to Piraeus. We became a Frugal Five after Barry left us on the way; of his own accord rather than being picked off by a bandit sniper! The displayed single ticket prices to Haifa were 8,500 drachmas, but we bargained it down to 7,200 drachmas. I probably wouldn't have made the effort on my own so I was well chuffed, although it didn't make up for taking the wrong ferry on the way over to Crete!

We left our rucksacks in the travel agency shop and chipped in 250 drachmas each for beans, tomatoes, pasta, bread and tea at a supermarket. Then we collected our bags and walked to the Paloma; our ship for the voyage. As we were sailing to Israel there was a stringent security check, and I blundered by telling the officer we'd left our bags at the travel agent. As this had given somebody the opportunity to plant something in our bags we had to empty them, and they searched the contents thoroughly. Moreover, none of us had an exit stamp from Greece, so we had to return to the Greek office and get one!

After all that we boarded and sailed at 4.30 p.m. We spent the early evening playing cards, cooking and eating, and ended it by watching *Death Squad*, which I didn't think was an appropriately titled film to show us with all the security concerns! I slept next to the others on the floor, and didn't wake through the night. Apart from a cold wind the weather seemed alright the next day, but we weren't allowed to disembark at Rhodes after arriving there at lunch-time. After leaving the port we sailed alongside Turkey for much of the afternoon, and there was a nice sunset in the evening. We played kaluki doubles for beers through the evening, and Lars and I beat the Derby boys 3-1; the competitive element brought a new tension to the game, and also more laughs, as Walter loudly blamed Zebedy for their defeats. I later wrote that during the cards I felt happier than I had while in the UK, as although I'd had good times at home the element of adventure and achievement felt from travelling and making new friends meant the intensity of the happiness seemed just that little bit higher. The sea got rough later on, and after bedding down I was half trying to sleep and half trying to stabilise myself!

I had a cold shower in the morning before sitting around with the others, writing my diary and reading *Mohicans*. Cyprus was visible for most of the morning, and we docked at Limassol in the early afternoon. The Frugal Five spent most of the two hours on the island having an English breakfast and large beer, which were delicious and very cheap. After leaving Limassol we played kaluki again before finishing the food. The sea was as rough as the previous night, but I found a couch to bed down on and it provided a great night's sleep.

The Guns N' Roses Worker-Traveller

The dawn of a new beginning in a continent I hadn't planned visiting when I left home beckoned the next morning. A land where sights, sounds and smells would fascinate and intoxicate me, but trouble would yet again never be far away.

Chapter 4

Mind-blown and Madness in the Middle-East: Israel and Egypt

We stirred as the ship entered Haifa harbour and disembarked after docking. Customs wasn't a problem; I received a three month visa and a big stamp, so was well chuffed. Ussi was going home and the others were returning to their kibbutz, so when I was approached by three men asking if I wanted to join a kibbutz I agreed. I goodbyed the others, and was especially sorry to leave Walter as he was a great laugh. It wasn't the last I'd see of him though, as we'd meet by chance later that year on Koh San road in Bangkok...but that's another story. I was joined in the mini-bus by two Swedes, Anders and Harald. We laughed about how kidnapping was a danger in the region and we'd got in the bus without knowing who the hell these people were. After leaving the harbour we stopped for food in Haifa before continuing south-east of Tel Aviv to kibbutz Ramat Hakovesh, situated between the Israeli and Arab towns of Kfar Saba and Tira.

We were met by a middle-aged woman called Roni, and after introductions she took us on a tour of the kibbutz: it looked impressive, with a gym, tennis court, shop, disco, dining hall and abundant greenery; the latter contrasting with the arid environment surrounding the grounds. Then we were allocated accommodation, and I was shown to a sparse room in the middle of a single-storey block. It contained two single beds, a table and chair, an old radio and an electric heater. There was a window at the front and back, with the former providing a view of some lawn and a two-storey block of volunteers' rooms. There was a small wood close to the

The Guns N' Roses Worker-Traveller

building at the back, and trees from it provided the only view from the rear window. My room-mate was called Bartholomew and he was British. He seemed friendly and had been on the kibbutz for a while, although he didn't have a good opinion of it. He took me up the dining hall for lunch, and I selected chicken legs, rice, sauce, salad and orangeade from the bountiful buffet. I thoroughly enjoyed it, and the thought of having nice food *on tap* for as long as I wanted was a tonic! The main meal was usually at lunch-time, and in the evenings there was only cold food; eggs, yoghurt and salad became my staples for the lesser meal. The meals switched around on the Sabbath, with the main meal in the evening.

On the first evening I sat with a group of volunteers who were to become my main friends on the kibbutz: Jasper and Ernie from Connecticut; a German called Mathias; two Colins, one from Guernsey and one from Southampton (to be known henceforth as Guernsey and Southampton), and Tyler from Vancouver. The conversation was pleasant and jocular, and I thought they were alright. However, nothing much happened after the meal, and I went to bed at 10 p.m.. It was quite cold at night, but there was a quilt on the bed, and using that and my sleeping bag made it warm enough to sleep naked. It had been quite an eventful day, with the kibbutz search easier than envisaged, so I felt good about life: I'd arrived on a new continent and was in a community for as long as I wanted, had a roof over my head, and a comfortable bed to sleep in.

I must have left the home comforts go to my head, as I slept a little too well; I didn't wake until 7:30, an hour after I was supposed to start grafting. I worked with Tyler in the kitchen and he was okay about my lateness. We had a good laugh all morning. Our main job was stacking dishes and cutlery after they'd been through an industrial washing machine, but there wasn't that much to do. We had breakfast and lunch with Candy and Spencer, a couple from Blackburn who were also working in the dining hall. After finishing work at 3 p.m. I joined in a kick-about with Guernsey and a Brazilian called Jao. A few others then joined us, and we played until it got dark. Southampton visited Bartholomew in our room after the evening meal and we drank some cheap vodka copy called wodka; it was only two shekels for a big bottle, and there were three shekels to the pound! There were some good tunes on the radio from the *Voice of Peace* radio station, including tracks from Aerosmith, Kiss, Def Leppard, Pink Floyd, U2 and Springsteen. However, the conversation never really developed, and I was relieved when Southampton left. Bartholomew continued talking, and was still going when I dropped off to sleep. Bartholomew and I both worked in the kitchen the next morning, with the chores similar to the previous day. At lunch-time I munched on falafel and pita bread for the first time and loved it. Ernie came to our room after work and tried to do the Jerusalem Post crossword with Bartholomew, but they got stumped and Bartholomew became manically irritated, reminding me of Rick from the *Young Ones.*

I settled into kibbutz life over the following days, and they passed without major incident; probably the most memorable event was a solo hike to Tira one afternoon, where the white-washed walls in an arid environment reminded me of villages in Greece, Spain and the Wild West. We beat some kibbutz members at football one night in the gym. Anders, who'd played semi-pro in Sweden, was the star of our team. The other volunteers who played were Felix from Argentina in goal, Jao, Bartholomew, Jasper, Guernsey, a South

The Guns N' Roses Worker-Traveller

African named Neil, and a German called Jurgen. Most of the volunteers who weren't playing were watching, which made for a good atmosphere. I mainly played in defence and made some impressive tackles, but didn't play that well with the ball at my feet. After similar displays on Crete I was beginning to think the silky skills of my youth had deserted me! On most of the nights we just chilled out around a fire on the lawn drinking wodka.

I'd been looking forward to Friday as it was the biggest day on the kibbutz, and we had Saturday off work. However, the anticipation still didn't get me up any earlier; Tyler and Linda woke me at 7, half an hour after I was supposed to start work! Linda was from Seattle and reminded me of Cissy Spacek. Work passed, and we started partying in Mathias' room after the evening meal. It was pucka having a big night again, and it seemed as if all the volunteers were in the vicinity. Harald, Anders and I drank a bottle of wodka each before going over the disco with the others. Once inside, Anders sneaked behind the bar to provide us with free drinks, while Bartholomew later had a fight with a kibbutz member. I couldn't remember the end of the night.

I spent the Saturday recovering, worked in the dining room on Sunday, and had a terrible day on Monday. The day started badly as I awoke late, and it just went downhill from there! I was down to work with the chickens and noticed the shed had a horrible acrid smell when I got there, so I didn't even want to enter. But begin I did, and my first job was to collect eggs from under the chickens. This entailed snatching shit-covered eggs from their mommas, with the indignant birds pecking at me the whole time; not only did I dislike the physical aspect of this, but I also felt guilty and thought they were justified in their actions! When the manager arrived he told us we should shower before working there, so I went home and had a long one! I returned to work until lunch-time, but the boss pissed me off afterwards and I walked out. I later gave Roni my reasons for jacking, and she seemed to accept them. I worked in the orange grove with Anders the day after, and being back amongst the citrus groves was a trip down memory lane!

I worked in the dining-room the rest of the week, and on Thursday night there was a meeting between the kibbutz leaders and volunteers to discuss our trip to the Dead Sea the next day. At the evening meal that night a volunteer called Rob was already drunk and messing about, and by the time the meeting started he was paralytic. The following hour became my funniest time on the kibbutz, as Rob booed and swore every time the kibbutz members tried to talk, causing the meeting to descend into anarchy.

We set off the following afternoon. Most of the others were drinking wodka but there was no mix on the bus, so I abstained. It also darkened soon after setting off, so I didn't see as much of the countryside as hoped. I still gazed out of the window, with the passing darkness and occasional bright lights reflecting my thought process. We travelled through the West Bank, where the Intifada was in full flow, and saw burning tyres *on the road*; the kibbutz members with us carried Uzis. We also travelled parallel with the Jordanian border, seeing movement from within a country that looked so near but was yet too far, as you couldn't cross into it from Israel at the time. We arrived at a car park next to the Dead Sea in the evening, and stayed there overnight. Being sober I didn't get into the party atmosphere, and went for a couple of walks around the area on my own. The members started a fire and we

The Guns N' Roses Worker-Traveller

barbequed some food. The flames seemed to attract some random people, but there was no hassle. I kipped at the side of the bus with the others, and slept okay considering the hard surface and not having a pillow.

We woke early, and after breakfast drove about ten miles along the Dead Sea valley to the bottom of Masada, a fortress from biblical times. We took a cable-car to the summit, and had a guided tour round the plateau and ruins; there was a great view of the desert, mountains and Dead Sea, and it was interesting historically, but there wasn't much left of the buildings. After about an hour we hiked down to the bus and set off for the Dead Sea. As we passed through the dry red rock desert several wild camels crossed the road in front of us and we stopped to let them pass; it was an amazing experience for me, and I became really enthusiastic for the first time on the trip. After a BBQ lunch most of us took a dip in the Dead Sea, which was also great. The water was warm, and it felt nicely weird floating on the surface; especially on a full stomach! I had the standard newspaper-reading photo taken, and remembered seeing such images as an incredulous child. After emerging from the briny and showering we bussed to an oasis and wildlife park called Ein Gedi, where we saw fresh-water springs, a waterfall and ibex.

That marked the beginning of the end for the trip, and we headed straight back to the kibbutz from there. I sat next to Ernie and we had a good conversation about our aspirations as we passed through mostly desert scenery. I think that whizzing through towns and villages, without knowing the intricacies contained within, to our comfortable kibbutz community made us laud travelling all the more, and we vowed never to stop. As you know, there had been times when the hobo life did not seem so appealing, but they were mostly forgotten at the time.

The next day brought the best weather since I'd arrived on the kibbutz, and after work we relaxed on the lawn and played basketball. I couldn't play very well with my injured wrist, and was made to look especially rubbish by some good North American players. Jasper later joined me for a run around the kibbutz as the sun set. We all got drunk on fruit punch at Neil's farewell party during the night; he was returning to South Africa.

I worked in the rubber components factory for the first time a couple of days later, starting at 7 a.m.. I worked with Linda, who was now with Tyler, helping her clip rubber bolts and clean the machines when they jammed. My life on the kibbutz plodded along for the next week or two, but Anders and Harald were asked to leave the kibbutz on the Saturday after missing work. I rose to bid farewell to the Swedes. Jao and two French-Canadians that shared the name Brigitte also left and I said goodbye to them too.

The surviving volunteers felt the Swedish expulsion had a hint of conspiracy about it when eight new volunteers turned up for the evening meal; it was kind of like everything was changing, with the troublesome generation of my arrival being replaced by a new one. However, there were some cool newcomers, and I had a good laugh with a couple of Canadians called Carl and Curtis. They joined us at a party in Guernsey's room later, and we initiated them into the wodka cult!

A few days later we had a fire going in the night and Bartholomew and I had a pissed-up argument, followed by him running into our room and throwing my clothes out. So I rose from the ground and ran towards our room, whereupon he shut the door, but I punched it with my right hand, knocking one of the panels out. I calmed down then, and the others followed me in to make sure everything was okay. We collected my clothes and got the panel back into place, but I'd punched the door with my crocked right hand, and it felt numb and weak.

I realised there was something seriously wrong with it the next morning as it had swollen, so I went over the clinic. They sent me to a hospital in Herzliya, and x-ray results showed I'd broken a bone in my wrist. They made me a plaster-cast that reached from hand to elbow and advised me to wear it for six weeks. Sahava put me on nights at the factory, which was generally regarded as the kibbutz punishment shift.

It curtailed my partying to a certain extent, but I still had a few drinks before starting work at eleven during the week and had Friday night off. I went to the disco with the others and left with Guernsey. He tried starting a water fight afterwards by chucking buckets of water on sleeping volunteers. Bartholomew and Mathias joined us, but some of the others weren't too happy about it and wanted revenge. They got it the following evening while Guernsey was at work, setting his bed and possessions out on the lawn. It was funny seeing him realise it was his bedroom out there upon his return! Roni lectured us about the wild parties and boozing on Monday, warning that people would be chucked off the kibbutz if it continued...so we boycotted the disco the following Friday.

During the week, I pierced my left ear through the cartilage on the corner, just above the lobe. The hole I originally made wasn't quite big enough for the stud to go through, so I asked the others for help, and

Marc Latham

Jurgen found a bigger needle to complete the job. I also received a hilarious letter from a seemingly despondent Ally in Platanias and a parcel from my mum containing a couple of Kerrangs and two tapes I'd requested. I borrowed a cassette player off Spencer to play the tapes, and it was great to hear Guns n' Roses, Scorpions and Rose Tattoo again, before Jurgen spoilt it by taking his lead back! We visited Tira to buy hash on Friday, but Jurgen wasn't happy with the deal, so we returned empty-handed. We had a lift back after sticking our thumbs out, which I counted as my ninety-seventh hitch of the trip. Jurgen, Jasper, Ernie, Tyler and Linda all departed on Sunday after Roni learned of a fire started on the floor of Tyler and Jasper's room, although they were ready to leave anyway. I'd also decided to leave the following weekend.

I did the night shift until finishing work on Friday morning, and spent most of the rest of the time playing cards with the others. I got drunk on Friday night at a party in Spencer's room before frequenting the disco. I couldn't remember the later stages, but was told that I cut my elbow after falling and it bled profusely. Mathias and Spencer carried me to my room and we smoked there until I crashed out. I recuperated in bed all the next day, but then couldn't sleep at night. I stopped trying after sunrise and spent the morning preparing to leave; I showered and packed, received fifty shekels and a kibbutz t-shirt off Roni, said goodbye to the others, and headed south after lunch.

I hitched from outside the kibbutz and had two lifts, taking my total to ninety-nine for the whole journey. However, I then got stuck at a bus-stop because there was a seemingly endless procession of soldiers appearing from somewhere, and they were always given preference for hitches by drivers; it must've been

The Guns N' Roses Worker-Traveller

near some barracks. I'd been there about an hour when a bus arrived, so I paid the five shekels fare and relaxed for the final sixty miles to Jerusalem.

We arrived just after dark, and as I walked round the centre I had mixed emotions about being alone for the first time in months; feeling about as free as can be and good to be out *on the road* again, but also with the pangs of loneliness that go with the territory. After settling down on a bench I started reading a new book I'd swapped on the kibbutz, *The Chinese Bandit*; it was about a western adventurer getting into trouble with local tribes while in East Asia. A Christian stopped to give me a sermon and bible, although I could've done with a bed more! Instead, it was behind the bushes again, and I got next to no sleep. I rose early and spent a cold and mostly cloudy day sightseeing, including visits to the Wailing Wall, Dome of the Rock, the military graveyard and the Holocaust memorial at Yad Vashem; I spent ages looking round the museum in the latter.

I didn't sleep well again that night, and bought a ticket to Eilat for fifteen shekels in the morning. The bus left at 2 p.m., and the temperature warmed as we travelled south through the Negev desert. It was already dark when we arrived in Eilat at about 7 p.m., but also nice and hot. One of the first people I saw in the centre was Anders, who was with another Swedish bloke he knew from home, Frankie. I spent the rest of the night with them at the Lido and (Red) Lion pubs, and Americana disco. We lost Frankie in the disco, but found him again in a hut where he and Anders had been sleeping; he was with a woman he'd pulled at the disco. She left after we arrived and the three of us slept there.

We were woken in the morning by workmen and quickly left. It was a blessing in disguise, as we emerged into a beautiful sunny day, and spent the rest of it on the beach and in bars. Most Israelis were on holiday for Purim, and in the evening we met Jao and Nedi from the kibbutz; they had a day off from the moshav they worked on. Nedi got paralytic and wandered off, and had been sick over himself when we found him. We helped Jao take him over the station, before they returned to the moshav. The Swedes were also drunk by the end of the night and doing their own thing, so I slept alone on the edge of the beach amongst the worker-traveller tent community. I didn't bother assembling my tent, and just slept in my sleeping-bag.

I spent the next morning on the beach, before frequenting the Lion after lunch; they showed a film each afternoon and had a Ramboesque movie set in the Middle-East on. I met Anders and Frankie there, and afterwards we went to the Lido and got drunk. At the end of the night I slept on the beach again, and vomited nearby! Rain woke me in the morning, and I rose despite having a hangover. The drizzle and early start gave me itchy feet, and after breakfast I hiked up to the Egyptian consulate, where a month's visa set me back 36 shekels.

I'd just returned to the beach when somebody called my name. I looked around and saw it was Tanya and Margot from Pirgos, so I walked over to them. Our meeting fulfilled mine and Tanya's hopes from the edge of Iraklion, but it was ironic that I'd just decided to leave Eilat! They said they'd left Crete for a moshav soon after we parted, and were now looking for work in Eilat. As I had a cast on my right arm they thought I'd been in trouble again, but I explained it was mainly a left-over from Pirgos. We reconvened at the Tropicana after a while and watched a film set in the Australian desert called *Earthling* while continuing to catch up with our

The Guns N' Roses Worker-Traveller

news; they said Michelle and Simon split up on the moshav after she got ill and he didn't take much notice. Margot left after the film but Tanya and I watched music videos, talked some more and had a laugh with some drunk travellers. I walked Tanya to their hostel at the end of the night and we talked and kissed as we had outside Talon's house on another continent. After she retired I returned to the beach and slept under the lifeguard's tower, as it'd been raining during the night. The girls met me on the beach in the morning and we stayed together until the late afternoon. When they left me we said our goodbyes again, as I was leaving to Egypt in the morning. It'd been nice to see Tanya again, albeit for a brief and final reunion.

I took a bus to the border at 8:30, and after paying twelve shekels in exit tax and twelve Egyptian pounds (EP) to enter Egypt I crossed without trouble; it was about four EP to a British pound. The Cairo bus was pleasantly modern and air-conditioned. I also had two seats to myself, so the ten hour journey was comfortable. After passing through a few towns and oases in the Sinai it was mostly arid desert, so I sent my gaze to the sand and let my mind wander across golden dunes to memories and dreams that lay just over the distant azure horizons; both the view and thoughts seemed to be constantly changing, but paradoxically also always remaining the same.

The weather worsened along the way and it was bucketing down when we reached Cairo. The rain, combined with darkness, noise, smells, bustle, and the excitement of being in such a different city made the atmosphere electric for me and I was buzzing. As I collected my rucksack two travellers that had been on the bus asked me if I wanted to share a taxi and room; one of them had a guide book and picked out the New

Cicil Hotel so we took a taxi there and rented a triple room for 13EP each. Mark and Brendan were both from New Zealand and had travelled extensively, but didn't know each other before Cairo. Mark was my age and meeting his girlfriend in Cairo, while Brendan was about thirty and on his last adventure before returning home. After settling in we went out for food and beer before calling it a day.

    I woke the next morning at 9 a.m. following a sound sleep. After a shower I went over to the tourist information office with Mark, before he went to find out about his girlfriend's flight. I strolled merrily along the Nile and through Ramses square to the train station, enjoying the hot sunny day. A first class ticket to Luxor for the following Sunday set me back 12EP. There was a jail next to the station and I saw shackled prisoners being unloaded from a van; as they entered sunlight for a few moments before being led away into darkness I appreciated my freedom all the more. After returning to our hotel and reuniting with the others we ate at a local restaurant. I had a dish called koshari, which is a delicious mixture of macaroni, rice, lentils and spices. A good chat finished the day off nicely, and as we walked back to the hotel I felt invigorated by the vibrancy of the city and the company of my room-mates.

    My first task of the new day was to replace my traveller's cheques at the American Express office, as they'd become rather dishevelled and I'd had trouble changing them. A bloke from our kibbutz was at the office, although he was one of the later recruits and I hadn't known him that well. Then I visited the city museum, which was only 3EP to enter and kept me occupied for most of the afternoon; the exhibits from Tutankhamen's tomb were the highlight. After returning to the hotel Brendan and I moved into a twin room, as

The Guns N' Roses Worker-Traveller

Mark was moving to a posher hotel with his girlfriend.

I registered with the government office the next morning, as required, before spending the day at the Pyramids and Sphinx, which exceeded expectations. I also went on a camel ride while there, sitting tandem behind the owner; it was a fun experience, although we didn't pick up too much speed! Although it was good to have ridden on a camel, the serenity of the setting, and enjoyment of the day were marred a little by people trying to sell you rides and mementos all the time.

It was already dark when I departed, so it became a little hairy trying to find my way back onto the main road through the ghettos of Giza. Matters weren't helped when a bloke in uniform called me over and motioned for me to join him in a sentry box only big enough for one, so I *exited stage left*. After finding the correct road I eventually got a free ride to the city in one of the mini-buses that drive round charging a little more than buses. Upon reaching the centre I took the tube to the Cicil's nearest station, but my mind and body were frazzled by then and I became disoriented after emerging into the night. A Eureka moment (or spark of common sense!) got me back on track and I was mightily relieved to reach the Cicil's hallowed doors and peace of mind!

I stayed in the city for the rest of the week and continued to have a good time visiting sites and socialising. Brendan had decided to leave on the same train as me, but he went out to the Sakkara pyramid in the morning, and we planned to meet later at the train station. My main task prior to catching the train was to get an international student card, as Walter said he bought his in Egypt, and I got one without much trouble for 6EP. Then I strolled round the mosques and citadels before making my way to the station via the hotel. I arrived way too early for once, so I decided to look for food. There was African Cup football on television in a nearby café, so I ate there and watched Morocco and Zaire draw 1-1 while chatting with a soldier. I got a bit engrossed in the football, and left at the last moment for the 8 p.m. departure; well, that's what I thought anyway, but when I returned to the station the train had gone! There was another at 8:30, but my ticket wasn't valid and there were no first class tickets available, so I bought second class for 6EP. I sat outside the toilets on the train, as it was full everywhere else, and read the *Chinese Bandit*. Then a beautiful Danish girl called Mette sat next to me and after we began conversing it became evident she also had a nice personality. She said she was travelling straight to Aswan with a couple from their kibbutz; they were seated in the next carriage. We got on great, although there were some locals with us most of the time, and they seemed fascinated with her. After a few hours I saw single seats had become available in the carriage, so I went in and we split. Mette had been reluctant to leave, and when *the penny dropped* I realised I'd blundered by separating myself from her!

We arrived in Luxor at noon and I said goodbye to Mette before disembarking. I was already kicking myself for leaving her, and felt like a mad dog or Englishman emerging into the midday sun; and the hottest day I'd ever experienced. There were also a lot of people about, and softened by my tiredness, the confusion and heat I quickly agreed to stay at the Atlas hotel after being offered a pillion ride there and a room for 5EP a night. After booking in I slept and ate before visiting the Valley of the Kings. You could see most of it from outside, so I wasn't going to enter, but then saw Brendan inside and paid the 1EP. You get a bit tight

The Guns N' Roses Worker-Traveller

when you're travelling in cheap countries, and usually start to value items in local currency: 1EP is a koshari meal and a couple of falafels! I also met an English bloke from the kibbutz called Henry inside, before reuniting with Brendan. He asked where I'd been, as he'd got the train we were supposed to share; my explanation of incompetence fulfilled his expectations! After leaving the site we watched the sun set over the Nile before finding a café to view Egypt's debut in the African Cup. There was a vibrant atmosphere at the one we chose, with chairs and tables spread out onto the pavement and into the road. You felt like the place would go crazy if Egypt won, or even scored, but a 1-0 defeat to Cameroon meant we never found out.

Brendan and I visited the Karnak temple the next day, but I didn't think it was that different to the Valley of the Kings, so I decided not to visit further temples. We also went over the Nile for a felucca trip, and joined a bloke from Guildford on a boat; he said he'd arranged to hire it for 15EP. We had a two-hour return journey to Banana Island for that and spent half an hour on the island, which not surprisingly featured banana plantations. It was nice and relaxing on the boat, but when we returned to Luxor and gave the felucca owner the money he asked for more. We refused to pay the extra and he started threatening us with an iron bar. We said we'd sort it out at the police station with him and walked towards it together, but as we neared the entrance he legged it.

Brendan and I took the bus to Aswan a couple of days later; it was the most southerly point of my journey, and I would start to slowly head home from there. After a comfortable four hours journey we booked into the cheapest hotel in town: the Continental. It was 1.5EP each a night in the four bed dormitory. We shared with a couple of blokes who'd been on a kibbutz and travelled through Egypt together: Conrad from Pittsburgh and Henrik from Stockholm. They were still in bed when we arrived at midday, so I thought we'd get on! Brendan and I walked round town in the afternoon, before watching the sun set over the Nile again. Dozens of vultures circled above it in the distance, adding drama to the natural beauty. We ended the day in the Aswan Moon, a boat restaurant on the Nile. We ate while watching African Cup football, with Egypt beating Kenya 3-0 to the locals' delight before Nigeria and Cameroon drew 1-1.

I enjoyed the easygoing culture promoted by heat-induced lethargy over the following days and just relaxed; I likened the Hotel Continental to the Eagles' *Hotel California*! Brendan visited the temple of Abu Simbel the next day, but it was quite a distance away and required a very early waking, so I gave it a miss. I woke late and talked with Conrad and Henrik until early afternoon, preferring to take it easy. Brendan returned in the afternoon and we all went out for falafels and a game of scrabble in the evening.

Whilst walking around town one day I met Mette's travelling companions; they said she was sleeping in the hotel. Although I'd been hoping to see her again I didn't want to disturb her, so I was gutted. Brendan and I met the guy from Guildford another time and he came back to our hotel for a party in the evening. It was a good night, with about twenty people having a smoke and playing music in a roofless upstairs hallway. The night-sky and constant heat provided extra dimensions to the sensory experience, and helped send the thought process into overdrive, while closing down communications.

The Guns N' Roses Worker-Traveller

I took the plaster cast off my arm the next day; my wrist felt fine, although it looked much smaller and whiter than the left. It meant I could write right-handed again, so updating the diary was much easier. The right hand hadn't forgotten how to write at all, but the left soon did! In the evening we watched Egypt's elimination, as they drew 0-0 with Nigeria when needing to win. There was disappointment amongst the locals of course, and especially as Egypt had the better of the game.

Conrad, Henrik and six others sailed north on a felucca the morning after, while Brendan left for the Sinai during the afternoon. The sudden solitude resulting from the loss of my chill-out buddies compelled me to visit Elephantine Island the day after. The majority population on Elephantine are Nubians, so it was a nice and interesting trip. I decided to leave after that, and as the journey down had been comfortable I bought a second-class ticket straight to Cairo. The train left in the evening again and I sat next to three men: two Sudanese and an Egyptian. It was okay, but I had little conversation. As the journey progressed I started a new book, *Plague Dogs*, about two dogs on the run from a research laboratory in the English Lake District. Then I slept until dawn, and afterwards mixed day-dreaming with dozing until arriving in Cairo at midday.

After eating at the station I made my way to the Oxford Pension; the cheapest traveller hotel in Cairo. I took a dorm bed there, and found it was in a worse state than the Continental! After dumping my bag I went out into the city. I bought three postcards and wrote them in the sun before posting them. Then I bought a bus ticket to a resort on the Sinai called Dahab, before buying an *Egyptian Gazette* and reading it while eating the second of two kosharis that afternoon. In the evening I watched

Barbarians and *Final Mission* at the cinema, and saw Mark and Donna sitting by the window in a restaurant while returning. So I reached in and jokingly grabbed their drink. After their initial shock we updated each other on our Egyptian adventures.

I left Cairo a couple of afternoons later; another modern bus departed punctually and I got some sleep after a soldier sitting next to me disembarked. We arrived in Dahab at 7.30 a.m. and I rented a hut with a bloke from Manchester called Zoots who'd also been on the bus. He was a seasoned worker-traveller and had been away from the UK for years. The hut was very basic, just consisting of walls and a concrete floor covered by mats, but was only 2EP each. I spent the day sunbathing before frequenting one of the tent-cafés on the beach for pizza, spaghetti and tea. The food was nice, but flies continuously tried to land on it, meaning you ate with one hand and swatted with the other. I met a German bloke I knew from the Aswan Continental called Manfred there, and Henry from the kibbutz came along later. We played backgammon and stayed until it closed at 11 p.m.. After returning to the hut I had a funny conversation with Zoots, who was already prostrate but awake, and *laughed out loud* at his tales of drunken antics *on the road*.

I spent the next day with Manfred and his hut-mate, an Israeli girl. They had snorkelling gear and I saw some good coral and fish using it, including the colourful multi-finned lionfish. Later, while eating a Tota restaurant happy hour half-price pizza I met a French bloke I'd vaguely known in Platanias; initially, we couldn't remember where we'd met before, and had to backtrack through our travels until reaching a common ground. The African Cup final was on television, with Cameroon beating Nigeria 1-0.

The Guns N' Roses Worker-Traveller

I also went to the Tota for breakfast, and after Manfred had joined me Conrad from the Continental also came along. C said he was sharing a cabin with Henrik in a nice location, so after eating we took a taxi over there and snorkelled in a nearby lagoon. After the sun set we returned to the main beach for supper in the Golden Sun, and I was delighted to see Mette walk in with the people she was travelling with. It was great to see her, and especially when she said *I knew I'd see you again* in a pleased tone. To end 48 hours of cool reunions Mark from Cairo later entered and we chatted.

Manfred, Conrad and Henrik left the next day, and I spent it with Mette and her companions. We had a nice day, but it all went downhill in the evening! I'd been telling them how much we'd smoked on the kibbutz, but then had the whities after a few tokes at her companions' tent and had to leave for fresh air and a lie down. My mind was in turmoil and my stomach churning, but I was more embarrassed than anything! Some passing Arabs enquired about my health as I lay on the sand. I said I was okay, but didn't feel it, and was relieved when they left me to my nightmare. I improved enough to re-enter the tent after a while, but wasn't much company in my nauseous state. Mette retired to her tent soon afterwards and I left a little later; an ignominious end to what had started out as a very promising day!

Mette and her friends asked if I'd like to travel to Israel with them the next morning, as they were leaving in a taxi, but I said I was staying on the Sinai for a few more days, as planned. It was my last chance to spend more time with Mette and I'd rejected it, which was the opposite of what I really wanted to do. I was sorry I hadn't suggested continuing to Aswan with her when we were on the train, as she'd seemed really happy we'd met again and it would have been great travelling with her in Egypt.

I spent most of the next day at the Golden Sun with some of the people who'd been at the Continental in Aswan. I put my Motley Crue, Guns n' Roses and Scorpions tape on their stereo, and swapped *Chinese Bandit* for a Vietnam War book, *Meditations in Green*. A couple of them had bad stomachs, and it hit me the next morning; it was bad timing, as I was due to travel north. I met the others at the Golden Sun for breakfast and then we went to catch our buses. I was travelling with an English male and female, Baloo and Indigo, up the coast to the smaller resort of Tarabin, while others were heading to Cairo and Taba. However, our bus was full when it arrived, and after waiting in vain and sickness all day for another one we ended up sharing a taxi with some other travellers.

Our delay did bring some good fortune, as we met Conrad and Manfred soon after arriving on Tarabin beach and they said we could stay with them as they had a big hut; Henrik had returned to the kibbutz due to sickness. So we made ourselves at home in their hut and the others started smoking. I was still feeling ill, so abstained and soon fell asleep. The signs weren't good the next morning, as I woke needing a shit and only liquid emerged, but I improved through the day. Baloo and Indigo also went down with it and Indigo had it bad. Conrad, Manfred and I visited the nearby village of Nuweiba in the afternoon and I had my first beer for three weeks while playing backgammon and darts. Manfred left for Cairo the next morning, while Conrad and I had a smooth journey through the desert and customs to Eilat. I hung round with him until he left for Jerusalem in the afternoon.

The Guns N' Roses Worker-Traveller

I was alone again...but it didn't last long, because as I strolled by the sea I came across a dozen people from the kibbutz. I met them where most of them were sleeping; in the middle of the beach. It was cool to see them all, and we quickly caught up on our news. They'd been working in Eilat for a few weeks, and a couple of relationships had developed: Curtis was with Marlene, a Danish girl, while Mathias was with an Englishwoman called Jenny. We later visited the Lion pub, where I integrated back into the beer culture by downing a gallon of the amber nectar, which went down extremely well. We talked and watched *Top of the Pops* tapes sent from the UK, which featured the Anthrax: *I am the man* and Aerosmith: *Dude looks like a lady* videos. After the pub I slept in my sleeping bag next to the others, as I couldn't be bothered assembling the tent for one night.

I awoke as the others prepared to look for work and walked up to the edge of Eilat with them before I continued to the northern highway. However, I didn't have any luck hitching, so I bought a bus ticket to Tel Aviv for fifteen shekels with my student card. It was sweltering on the bus, as there was no air-conditioning. From Tel Aviv it took three bus rides to reach the kibbutz and it was evening by the time I arrived. Seeing people around a fire on the grass brought back fond memories of our boozy gatherings.

After joining them I met some new volunteers and a few of the oldies, like Southampton and Guernsey. Henry had also returned after Egypt and I stayed in his room, as there was a spare bed. After dumping my rucksack we frequented the dining room for sustenance and a chin-wag; he said Bartholomew had left for Eilat that day. I saw Roni there and she said she'd sent my mail back as she didn't think I was returning, which was a downer. However, the next day I learnt there was one letter that a volunteer had kept, so after collecting it I read it in H's room. Although I was initially happy to receive the letter it contained bad news, as my mother wrote that my grandmother had died. She'd been the only grandparent I knew, as her husband was killed in World War Two and my mother was adopted. We hadn't been that close, and a postcard sent from Cairo was the first time I'd contacted her for ages. Ironically she'd died before that, so wouldn't have received it. I was therefore sorry I hadn't sent one earlier, as I would have liked her to have received something from me before she went. The evening was uneventful, but I had asthma and diarrhoea in the night and needed the toilet a few times. The surgery gave me tablets for the latter in the morning, and after breakfast goodbyes I made my final exit from the kibbutz.

    I had a lift with the kibbutz bus to Kfar Sava and took buses from there to Tel Aviv and Eilat. On the latter I sat next to an Israeli who worked in the radar station in Eilat; we had a good chat and she shared her chocolate, crisps and orangeade. After arriving I hiked to where the others had been staying on the beach and found Spencer, Bartholomew, Curtis and a few others. It was funny catching up with Bartholomew, who was delighted to have escaped the kibbutz. However, Carl and some others had gone to Egypt, while Mathias and Jenny had left that day for a Moshav; the latter later returned after trying to hitch without luck for seven hours, but went the next day. The others helped assemble my tent near Spencer and Candy's in the tent community, before we ate spaghetti and sauces the group cooked on the beach. Our bellies full, we washed it down with beer while playing darts in the Lion. At the end of the night I returned to where the majority were

The Guns N' Roses Worker-Traveller

sleeping until everybody started bedding down, and then slept in my tent for the second time of the trip!

After awakening at first light I joined the others. Once everyone was ready we ambled up to the Peace (Café), the work-café in Eilat. It was quite a walk from the beach, and mostly uphill! We arrived at 6:45 but it didn't look promising. As it was Passover there didn't seem many employers around and the workers-wall was already full. However, I soon got a restaurant job, although it only paid four shekels an hour; the average for Eilat seemed to be five. I initially worked with a Palestinian doing odd jobs around the place, like squeezing oranges for juice, peeling potatoes and cleaning, but when customers started eating I was mainly washing dishes. I worked until 8 p.m. and it was alright, as I had drinks when required and three good meals. I also ate unfinished food off plates if it looked clean and appetising! I met Spencer and Curtis on the beach after work and we had a look around a fair that was in town before crashing out. The diarrhoea and asthma that had troubled me on the kibbutz had cleared, and I never had any asthma problems in Eilat again, probably because of the dry conditions. Being healthy and having a job while living in a sunny beach community meant I was upbeat about life, and any worries about looking for work in Israel had disappeared; the only regret I had was not leaving the kibbutz earlier.

I worked at the restaurant until 11 p.m. the next day, and was on my own until 3 p.m.; I was knackered afterwards and went straight back to the tent. I met Dominique, the French-Canadian I knew from Crete on the beach the next morning. We spent a while catching up with our travelling news until I left for work. I toiled from 10 a.m.-11 p.m. again and was on my own until the

Palestinian arrived for the night. As it was the last day of the holiday it was also very busy. I met Bartholomew and Zoots in the Lion after work, and had a laugh.

When I told the others about my work hours and rate the next morning they recommended that I jack the job, as there was plenty of construction work around with better hours and pay. It was in line with my thinking anyway, as I was sick of finishing late. Another long, stressful day intensified the feelings, and at the end of the shift I resigned and got paid up. I celebrated my freedom with Zoots, Dominique, Curtis and Bartholomew in the Lion.

However, my *brave new world* didn't start well the next day as I didn't get work, and left the Peace with Bartholomew after a few hours. It was a hot sunny day, so after buying food and checking for post we joined some of the others on the beach. Any second thoughts I had about ditching the restaurant job were soon forgotten as I revelled in the beach life: chatting, sunbathing and swimming. Moreover, we cooled off in the afternoon with a few pints in the Lion. They had *Down and Out in Beverly Hills* on, and we watched that before frequenting the Hard Rock café; a small bar-restaurant near the Peace owned by a cockney bloke rather than the big multinational. While sitting by the bar I got talking to a couple of blokes, Barney and Worm from Cambridge, and it turned out that not only had they been on our kibbutz after I left, but they also knew Zoots from working together on mainland Greece! Moreover, I also met a girl who'd been in Pirgos the same time as me!! The Hard Rock provided British food, and on good work days we'd usually have curry, while on lean ones we'd happily make do with egg and chips.

My decision to ditch the dishes job was

financially vindicated the following day, after I got two construction jobs; the first was only for a couple of hours, but the second lasted a few days. On the latter I worked with a bloke called Hoody preparing a backyard for concreting at a nice villa. It was five shekels an hour and nice to be working out in the sun, with a good view over Eilat and the sea to boot.

After the second day's work I met up with some of the others at the Lion, but all the pubs closed at 7 p.m. as it was Holocaust Remembrance the next day. So we went down to the beach and were strolling along it when I saw someone that resembled Ally from Platanias on it, and after a closer look realised it was him. After recovering from the shock I made myself known to him, and he seemed as surprised to see me as I'd been him. The others carried on walking while we caught up with our news: Ally'd left Platanias a fortnight ago with Joe and they'd been on a kibbutz since, but Ally didn't like it and left; Joe'd injured his leg and was still there. We couldn't celebrate our reunion with a few pints as all the pubs were closed, so we joined the others on the beach and I introduced him over a couple of cans. Ally slept amongst them after I returned to my tent.

Ally left his rucksack in my tent the next morning before going up to the Peace, while I walked in the opposite direction with Spencer, who was working near me. While making our way up the hill we heard a thud, and looking skyward saw a pigeon plummeting to the ground while a hawk turned in flight above it. After an easy half day in work, preparing steel for concreting, I returned to the beach and updated my diary before joining the others. We went up to the centre in the evening, but had to wait until 8 p.m. for Remembrance Day to end and the pubs to open; once inside the Lion,

Marc Latham

Ally and I celebrated our reunion properly by getting drunk.

I was hung-over in the morning, and was grateful to have an easy time at work, just spreading concrete poured from a lorry. I did it in bare feet as I didn't want to finish off my decrepit trainers. After finishing at lunchtime I lazed around with the others; it was Spencer's birthday, and we celebrated with punch on the beach and beer in the Lion. I was blotto by the end, and the next morning found sick in my tent. I was later told that Bartholomew had pulled my shorts down in the middle of the Lion and I'd fallen off a bar stool!

I finished off with Hoody on Monday and met the others after work; they said a police patrol had moved them from the middle of the beach, so they'd relocated to the tent community. Ally put his rucksack in my tent the next morning, and as he was supposed to return before me I let him put a padlock on the zips. I got employed soon after arriving at the Peace by a bloke called Moshe, and worked alongside an Englishman named Andy; we moved building materials and mixed cement for six shekels an hour. We had a good day, and after finishing at 3.30 p.m. were pleased to hear there was more work for us in the morning. I joined the others on the beach, and after swimming, sunbathing, shaving and showering we frequented the centre for food and drink. I spent most of the night talking to a woman called Raquel who'd been on our kibbutz after me, and at the end of the night we walked to the tents ahead of the others. After half a year of celibacy I thought I was definitely going to score, and had a clear path to goal, but when we arrived at the tent I found it was still locked, and Ally was nowhere to be seen. The others joined us soon after, and following a bit of ribbing about what we were up to the opportunity was lost, and

The Guns N' Roses Worker-Traveller

I'd missed another chance!

Another hang-over followed the next morning, and it wasn't helped by working for twelve hours on a sweltering day. I was knackered by the end, so when Moshe paid us for the two days and said there was half a day left for one person I was happy for Andy to have it. I felt faint by the time I reached my tent and decided to take the next day off before crashing out. I rose at about 10.30 a.m. and noticed my feet were swollen; I thought it must have been because of concrete or flies infecting the cuts on them. I spent the day sunbathing, swimming, reading *Meditations* and talking with some of the others; most only worked until lunch-time, as it was the eve of Israel's Independence Day and most employers finished early. We frequented a packed Lion in the night, and had the usual good night of boozing.

I recovered the next day, and on Friday worked with a bloke who'd employed me before. We drove thirty miles into the desert and spent the day carrying tiles from his lorry into the basement of a house they were building. It was easy work, and we got six shekels an hour and food, so I considered it a good day's business. Ally and I worked with him on Monday at the same house, shovelling chippings this time. After returning to the centre I changed some shekels for deutschmarks, as I was preparing for a return to Europe, and then we found a bar showing the League Cup final: Luton went 1-0 ahead against Arsenal, but the Gunners came back to lead 2-1, before the Hatters eventually won 3-2. There was a large crowd of worker-travellers in the bar, including one Arsenal supporter, so the banter was a good laugh. After returning to the tent Spencer gave me penicillin tablets for my feet, as they were worsening if anything. I started the course straight away, but dreaded having to abstain from alcohol!

Marc Latham

I had a good laugh with an Englishman called Adrian on two jobs the next day; the first was the usual building work, but the second was more interesting, as we helped a crane driver manoeuvre massive boulders into position for a bomb-shelter. It was heavy work when we got going, but we just stood around most of the time, and could only do so much with the rocks anyway. We also did a few hours on the bomb-shelter the next morning, and after work met Carl from the kibbutz; he was passing through Eilat after returning from Egypt. The three of us went to a pub called The Pub and watched the film, *Over the Top*. I couldn't drink to our reunion because of the penicillin, so it was bad timing in that regard.

My feet had healed a couple of days later so I stopped taking the penicillin, and the old amber nectar sure did taste sweet that night! Ally and I worked alongside two Scots, Angus and Steve, and an Englishman, Ian, the next morning. The job was a good laugh, unloading boxes of ice-creams into an industrial freezer at a factory. We worked as a chain, with Steve and I as the freezer links, while the others were out in the sun. It was of course freezing inside, but they provided warm clothes and it was quite nice to have a respite from the heat. We received twelve shekels and a box of ice-creams for a couple of hours work, and then returned to the Peace together for a few pints. We had a great laugh before Ally and I got another job without trying; although I'd been reluctant to leave the café it turned out to be worthwhile, as we received ten shekels and a beer each for an hour's work.

The work situation didn't look promising at the Peace the next morning, as a melon-picking job had fallen through and there were about twenty worker-travellers on the wall. However, I was one of the first to

The Guns N' Roses Worker-Traveller

get a job, and worked alongside some Palestinians, a Dutch bloke and a British guy called Tazzy. We had a comfortable time loading and unloading pick-ups at a warehouse, and after finishing at 2 p.m. we each got 42 shekels. We frequented the Hard Rock with Ally and Bartholomew, and were joined by Barney and Worm before relocating to the Peace for a few more pints. Then we walked down the Lion and met Tazzy there, before a fight broke out between Tazzy's friends and another group of worker-travellers. Ally and I joined in with Tazzy's mates, and as the ruckus escalated it spread out onto the court. I ended up fighting a giant who picked me off as I swung at him, but I kept going until everyone scattered when the police arrived. There were no arrests at the scene, and nothing untoward ever occurred between the two groups again. Bartholomew later said Ally and I were the talk of the worker-traveller community because we'd punched above our weight and fought tenaciously, so that felt good, although I didn't think I'd done well really.

As the kibbutz community had taken a turn for the worse before my departure, the Eilat community was also now declining; only Bartholomew remained of the original kibbutzees, as temperatures soaring above 40c meant there was less work. However, I got a few days construction work during the week for six shekels an hour. On the Friday I was paid up for one job in the morning and got work with Ally after lunch. The employer said he'd pay us 25 shekels each to move heavy building materials, probably thinking it would take four hours. After he left us to it we blitzed it in under an hour and then just sat around waiting for him to return. He arrived an hour later, but when he saw we'd already finished he didn't want to give us the full 25; we insisted it was piece work and he paid up in the end. Then, after returning to the Peace, we got a job with Bartholomew moving boxes of wine. We initially agreed a price of fifteen shekels for the job, as they said it would take one and a half hours, but after an hour we realised it was going to take much longer. After telling them our concerns they agreed to an hourly payment rate, so we continued working and finished the job, but when we knocked on their door two British blokes living in the house told us the owners had left and they didn't know when they'd return. We didn't want to wait indefinitely, so we took three boxes of wine in payment for the work, and one of the residents provided a lift to the beach. We'd already been drinking wine as we worked, and continued on the beach while trying to sell the rest.

I felt rough the next morning, but made it up to the Peace with Ally and Bartholomew. They said I'd been falling into people and being abusive while selling the wine, but we'd made about eighty shekels. Apparently we were the talk of the worker-traveller community again! After positioning ourselves on the wall the employer Ally and I had hassle getting money from the previous day offered us work but we turned him down. I later got employed to mix concrete for a new floor, and had an okay day's work.

I returned to the beach afterwards and sat with the others while they drank wine; I abstained because I still felt hung-over from the previous day. Ally had received bad news from home during the day, and went for Bartholomew after he was annoying. Once Worm and I realised Ally was serious we jumped in to separate them. They later made up in the Lion.

I worked with the same bloke as the previous day in the morning, levelling out a garden for six shekels an hour. After work I moseyed down the Lion and watched the last hour of *Midnight Express* with Ally and

The Guns N' Roses Worker-Traveller

Barney; as I was soon visiting Turkey the film was quite worrying! We spent the afternoon on the beach, and in the evening called at Christian John's for free food. It consisted of beans and rice, and was both edible and filling. Then we ambled over to the Peace for a couple of pints, before visiting the Lion for a few more. There seemed to be an edgy atmosphere there, and a few fights broke out during the night.

The Saturday turned into an all day drinking session after we woke late and didn't look for work on another sweltering day; and kept meeting people we knew! It started when Ally and I encountered a Geordie and a Scouser in the supermarket and didn't need much arm-twisting when they invited us up to the Peace. Tazzy and his mates joined us there and we all went to the Neviot afterwards, where there were more Brits from the beach. After several beers and a great laugh we moved to the Red Rock, and met up with Barney and Zoots there. I was pissed by the evening and crashed out back at the tent.

A South African called Justin got me a job mixing cement and carrying bricks with him at six shekels an hour the next morning. We worked until 8 p.m., although we had an hour for lunch and a two-hour break from 3.30. After the boss paid us 55 shekels each I headed towards the Peace, but after meeting Ally, Bartholomew and some of the others coming down from it I went to the Lion with them. We called at the Tropicana on the way, as they gave a free half pint between 9 and 9.10 p.m., and we were bang on time. Bartholomew said he was going home in a couple of days after having money sent over for a flight. I also planned on leaving for Turkey the following week, bringing an end to our kibbutz group's presence in Eilat.

Marc Latham

I began my last week's work with a nice job in the King Solomon hotel, getting paid 33 shekels and having a free lunch in the air-conditioned cafeteria. After returning to the beach I updated my diary with flies continuously irritating me, and then spent the afternoon sunbathing and swimming. I later visited the usual haunts with Ally, and met up with some people along the way; including Justin, who offered me work for the morning.

So I worked with him and his boss again the next day, before having a few beers in the Lion while watching *Platoon*. There was also supposed to be work with them the next day, but Justin didn't turn up in the morning and his boss didn't want to work without him. So I returned to the Peace and got another job, but the employer seemed dodgy when I arrived at the site, so I walked off. I returned to the Peace but didn't get another offer, so had a day off after thinking I had two jobs along the way! I wasn't too bothered, as it was a scorching day and I spent the afternoon watching *Crocodile Dundee* and a Bronson vigilante film in the Lion.

I made up for it the next day as I got 84 shekels from twelve hours work; laying out blocks and polystyrene alongside an Irishman called Aidan. We worked there again the next day, and got paid up to lunch despite lying in the sun on the polystyrene for much of the morning! Our boss gave us a lift back to the Peace and we had a pint there before frequenting the Lion, where we watched an episode of *Minder*. Then I went down the beach for a swim and shower.

As I took in the sunset turning the Jordanian hills from pale yellow to orange and red across the shimmering blue sea for the last time, I thought back to all the good times we'd had in Eilat; I'd loved the time on the beach, and was sorry to be leaving. Jordan looked so close across the bay, but yet was unreachable to us; although according to Eilat worker-traveller legend one drunken hobo rowed over in a canoe before getting picked up by the Jordanian security and returned. In many ways, that story summed up the hardcore Eilat worker-traveller community: drunken but ingenious, mad but resourceful.

After getting drunk on Friday night we struggled to the supermarket on Saturday morning for an early start; the FA Cup final was being shown on television, and we were making a day of it! We sat out in the sun drinking and having a laugh, and I was drunk by the time we frequented the Lion for the game. I couldn't remember anything about the match the next morning, and the others said I slept through most of it. Wimbledon beat Liverpool 1-0 in one of the biggest upsets of all time, so it would have been good to watch, and I also lost my *Monsters of Rock* t-shirt, but I'd had a good morning!

I wasn't going to work on my last day in Eilat but then decided I'd might as well, as nobody else was off. I bought a bus ticket to Tel Aviv on the way up to the Peace, before doing my last worker-traveller job of the trip; working on construction alongside an Englishman called Pete from 7:30-11 for 28 shekels and a baguette. We frequented the Peace and Lion after work, and in the latter watched one of my favourite films, *For A Few Dollars More*, which was quite appropriate considering I'd worked on my last day in Eilat when I hadn't intended to! Justin was there as well, and I chatted with him before saying goodbye. Then I went down to the beach to collect my gear, before making my final trek up to the centre with Ally; I left the tent standing on the beach. Some of the others were in the Lion and we had a good laugh before I said numerous farewells. Ally left the pub the same time as me and we said our final goodbye; I'd hear from him again, but that was the last time I saw him. I walked up to the station and boarded the midnight and thirty bus. After leaving Eilat I slept for most of the journey, and woke in Tel Aviv.

Chapter 5

Homeward Bound via Turkey, Eastern Europe, Austria and Germany

We arrived in Tel Aviv at about 5 a.m.. When the local bus service started I got one into the city to buy an Istanbul ticket; after enquiring at a few travel agents I purchased a single for about £100, paying with 161 shekels and 70 deutschmarks (DM). Everything was running smoothly, but I might have known it wouldn't last, and I had a nightmare going through security after returning to the airport. They asked me to take the canister out of my stove, but as I tried unfastening it the gas started releasing loudly and everybody in the vicinity looked over in a panic as if a bomb had exploded! Needless to say, I was again very embarrassed!!

Despite the calamitous interlude I boarded the plane and had an uneventful flight sat next to an Aussie bloke; we left at about 2.30 p.m. and arrived in Istanbul a couple of hours later. I had no trouble getting through security, and then changed £20 at the airport for 49,000 Turkish lira (TL) at about 2,000 TL to a pound. I linked up with five other travellers outside the airport and we took a bus to the Yucelt youth hostel on the Sultanahmet peninsula; a dorm bed was 5,200 TL. After settling in I washed some clothes and talked with a pleasant dark-haired woman from Wolverhampton called Helen. I later ventured out for a meal at the Vitamin restaurant, and had a conversation with an Iranian who spoke good English. I returned to the hostel and bed at about 11 p.m.; after weeks of sleeping in the tent under extremely hot conditions it was a pleasure to kip in a cool room and comfortable bed.

I spent the next morning updating the diary and planning my Turkish travel, and the afternoon sightseeing: I visited the Topkapi Palace and the Blue Mosque, walked along the Bosporus and over the bridge from Europe into Asia, and took the ferry to the far side of Istanbul. A local paid for my return trip. During my jaunt I met a Brit I vaguely knew from Platanias and Eilat; I couldn't remember his name, and didn't think he knew mine, but we'd basically followed the same worker-traveller circuit for the last six months! I returned to the hostel in the evening and talked with Helen and her sister, Cynthia, while watching music videos. They were taking the same route as me the next day so we arranged to travel together.

We took a bus to the Topkapi terminal in the morning and each bought a 6,000 TL ticket for the 2 p.m. bus to Cannakkale. The bus didn't leave until 3 p.m., and by the time we left Istanbul the aisle was full of passengers. You could tell the aisle wasn't supposed to be occupied because every time we passed a checkpoint or police car the people ducked down! The journey went smoothly, and we reached Cannakkale at 9 p.m. after taking a ferry across the Dardanelles Strait; again passing from Europe to Asia. We found a cheap hotel and took a triple room for 2,000 TL each before going out for food. There was a television in the restaurant showing the UEFA Cup final second leg, with Bayer Uerdingen beating Espanol 3-0 to level the aggregate score, and then winning 4-3 on penalties.

My breathing was wheezy in the morning and I took puffs on my asthma inhaler; the climate was wetter in Turkey than Eilat, and the change in conditions seemed to have affected my chest. The girls visited

The Guns N' Roses Worker-Traveller

Troy during the day, but I'd heard there wasn't much to see so I didn't bother. I walked up a nearby hill for a good view over the town instead. After returning to the hotel and reuniting with the girls I took them up the hill, as they'd wanted to visit it after hearing about it. Viewing over, we were hiking back to town when a local with an Aussie accent started talking to us outside a carpet shop. He introduced us to a middle-aged Irish bloke called John, and the owner of the shop, Mehmet, and invited us inside. We had a good chat over beer and raki, before they took us to a restaurant for food and more drinks. A Canadian-Turk called Nick, a Swiss-Indonesian named Ralph and a young Turk, Samil, also joined us, and after the restaurant closed we went to Samil's room until 2 a.m. for more drinks with him and Ralph.

We called at the shop to thank them for the previous night and say goodbye in the morning, but they insisted on making a day of it, and took us to a museum and war memorial before buying us a meal. Then we said farewell again before making our way over to the station for the night-bus to Izmir. We couldn't find seats at first, but then the conductor found the girls some in the back of the bus and me one in the middle. After the generosity of the people in Cannakkale I thought he was another nice bloke, but after disembarking the girls said he'd tried molesting them.

We were pissed off about it but cheered up soon after, as we amazingly bumped into Samil from Cannakkale while looking for a hotel; he was on a delivery job, and helped us find a room. We had tea and a chat with him afterwards, before saying goodbye again. The highlight of the rest of the day was buying a pair of plastic baseball shoes for 13,500 TL.

The girls and I were travelling in different directions the next morning, so I paid my share of the bill after breakfast and bade farewell to them. I had a kiss on the cheek off Helen, and thought that if she'd been alone something might have developed between us. Who knows?

I took a dolmus to the terminal and a bus to Kusadasi. I was looking for a hotel after arriving when I met Raquel, the woman I took back to my tent in Eilat. She was with a South African girl who'd also been on the kibbutz after me. After talking for a while I continued searching for cheap accommodation, but when I couldn't find any I left for Efes; the historic site was the main reason for visiting the area, and it was only a few miles away.

I hitched in motion out of town without success, but as I passed a secluded hut a man invited me to drink tea. There was another man inside making marble statues, and after agreeing to their offer they made me tea and fried eggs. It was a nice spot, with just open countryside around, and I enjoyed relaxing under a hot sun. So when they brought some wine out I was happy to continue socialising with them, although they couldn't speak much English and were trying to sell statues, coins and other stuff a lot of the time. It was a strange evening, and the situation seemed to take control of my senses; I kept on meaning to leave but stayed rooted to the spot, and when they later offered me a sleeping place on the floor of the one-room hut I accepted. I knew anything could happen, and slept with my rucksack between myself and the wall, but got off to sleep after a while and woke the next morning unharmed. They made tea before I left, and after supping it with them I took some photos before continuing to Efes. I paid 2,000 TL to enter the Greco-

The Guns N' Roses Worker-Traveller

Roman site, and enjoyed the impressive architecture inside; moreover, a folk group played in the amphitheatre, bringing life to the history. After seeing my fill I walked to Selcuk, took a bus to Denizili for 3,000 TL, and then dolmussed to Pamukkale.

I rented a room with an Australian called Logan for 3,000 TL each. He put my Rose Tattoo tape on his hi-fi after I mentioned being a fan of the Aussie band. Then I visited the white calcium pools on the mountainside, which turned out to be one of the best sights of the trip, with water flowing down rocks that resembled snow or ice from afar. I sat in one of the pools and it was totally idyllic looking out over the sun-kissed green valley from the warm water and beautiful surroundings. I accompanied Logan and three English girls he'd met to a restaurant in the evening; the women were nice, but a bit posh, with one at Oxford University. Logan left the next day after breakfast. While we ate an old local got us a beer and was very interested in my tattoos. I paid to enter an outdoor pool near the calcium rock afterwards, and spent a couple of hours swimming and relaxing in the warm natural water on another sunny day. There were Roman-style stone pillars in the water, and the pool provided a nice view of the serene surroundings. I left the next day, but had a nasty shock when I received the bill, as they'd included 750 TL for the beer the old man got us; it was too small an amount to argue about, and I'd enjoyed the beer, so I just paid it.

I dolmussed back to Denizili, and bought a bus ticket to Fethiye for 4,000 TL. A spectacular five hours mountain journey ensued, and after reaching Fethiye I dolmussed to the smaller resort of Olu Deniz. The latter surpassed all expectation, as it was situated in a small cove with azure water and fine white sand. Rhodes was out at sea a little further up the coast, so I was now on one of the beaches visible from the Athens-Haifa ferry four months before, when we were all getting seasick! I had another blast from the past as I hiked along the beach looking for accommodation, because I met the Aussie seated next to me on the plane to Istanbul. He was with two girls and showed me a roof dormitory they were staying at for 1,500 TL each. So I took a bed there and met some other residents: three lads from Bristol called Pongo, Jermaine and Maggle; and a couple from New Zealand, Steve and Sally. Steve and I found a bar showing the European Cup final in the evening and had a few beers; the game between PSV and Benfica ended in a boring 0-0 draw, with PSV winning 6-5 on penalties. Steve got drunk and fell off his chair, before nearly having a fight with a local who tried to quieten him. After returning to the roof he and Sally kept us awake for ages arguing like a *dog and cat on a hot tin roof.*

I stayed in Olu Deniz for four days and had a thoroughly enjoyable and drunken time. We'd usually sunbathe during the day before retreating to the roof for some beers in the afternoon. It clouded over one morning so we started drinking early, and only left the roof to buy more beer. I didn't remember doing it, but apparently I downed half a bottle of vodka in one glug that night. On my last morning I said my goodbyes before dolmussing back to Fethiye. I bumped into Pongo again in Australia and Thailand, and needless to say we were out boozing both times!

I travelled eastward to Antalya from Fethiye, before taking a night bus to Nevsehir, in Cappadocia; I was fortunate to catch the latter bus, after thinking it departed two hours later than it did! Moreover, I had a double seat to myself and got some sleep, although it was still quite uncomfortable. We arrived in Nevsehir at about 7 a.m. and I slept for a few hours after finding a

The Guns N' Roses Worker-Traveller

dorm bed for 2,000 TL. There had been a couple of local looking men in the dorm when I arrived, but I awoke in an otherwise empty room.

I got a map and info from the tourist office, and started hiking out to Derinkuyu; I met an Australian couple on the way and we walked round the spectacular underground city together. After returning to Nevsehir I bought an envelope for my diary, letters and mementos, and posted them home for 5,000 TL. I also sent four postcards, including one to Ally in Eilat. I later walked up to the castle for a good view over the town and read some *Meditations*; yes, I was still working my way through what wasn't exactly easy reading!

I dolmussed to Goreme the next morning, and took a bed in another shared room. I saw there was amazing scenery all around, and went for a walk straight away. As I strolled among a plethora of rock towers reaching to the horizon, and stretching my imagination even further, my childhood memories of incredible other-worlds came flooding back. Invigorated, I climbed into the open-air museum for a look around, saving the 2,000 TL entrance fee, before walking three miles to Ortahisar, and ascending the natural rock tower for a great view. I later hiked to Uchisar, seeing more stupendous scenery on the way, and an awesome rock castle in the town.

I dolmussed back to Nevsehir the next morning and tried hitching from there, but didn't have any luck; I was stuck on my ninety-ninth hitch! So I walked back into town and bought a ticket to Ankara for 4,500 TL. The scenery was mundane on the journey and I read a *Turkish Daily News* most of the time. After arriving four hours later I bought a ticket for the 10 p.m. bus to Istanbul, and passed the intervening time walking through Lunar Park and reading *Meditations*. We left on time and I had a good journey, as I was by the window, got some sleep and had a friendly local next to me.

We arrived in Istanbul at about 6 a.m. and I took a bed in a small pension I'd been told was cheaper than the hostel. There didn't seem to be anyone else staying in my dorm, and I talked with the owner before going out for a walk. I enquired about a bus ticket to Munich in a few travel agencies, but didn't buy one as they all seemed to be 35,000 TL, and I thought I might find one cheaper later. We'd be passing through Bulgaria on the journey and a visa was required, so I went to the consul next. I paid 13,000 TL for the visa and got talking to a British couple called Eddie and Jane while waiting for it to be processed. Eddie had a funny tattoo of a bear-mermaid on his arm, and thought it humorous himself. After getting the visa and saying goodbye to the couple I bought a 'Lacoste' t-shirt for 5,000 TL and three pairs of 'Nike' and 'Adidas' socks for 3,000 TL at the Grand Bazaar. There was a downpour at the time, so it was packed and vibrant inside. On the way back to the pension I bought and ate a punnet of peaches, forcing me to rush back for the toilet! After relieving myself I updated the diary before going to a posh hairdressers; the first proper cut of the journey. It cost 5,000 TL, and they shampooed it beforehand. It turned out okay, but it was a little short in the front and I lost an earring! Newly shorn, I returned to the travel agents and paid 35,000 TL for a next day ticket to Munich. I met Eddie and Jane in the vicinity, and we went over the Blue Mosque sound and light show. However, we didn't think much of it, so we bought some beers and had a good laugh drinking them in a nearby park; some tramps joined us for a while, and others scuffled across the street. The doors were locked when I returned to the pension, and I had to knock to enter.

The Guns N' Roses Worker-Traveller

I passed time in the morning and early afternoon, and then had to wait a little longer than expected for my departure, as company bungles meant we had to get the 5 p.m. bus instead of the scheduled one at 3 p.m. That wasn't the end of our troubles however, as tyre trouble on the edge of Istanbul meant another couple of hours delay. After finally leaving Istanbul we settled into what promised to be a memorable journey. All the seats on the bus were full, and there were people sitting all the way down the aisle. There were only westerners on the back seat, with a Swiss guy, Bernhard, on my right, and an Irish bloke called Martin and an American couple on my left

A few hours later we arrived on the border with Bulgaria and had a passport check. There was no toilet on the bus, so it was also a restroom stop, but there was a small charge to enter and I didn't have any Bulgarian money. I thought I'd have to return to the bus in discomfort, but a local saw my plight and paid for me. As the journey progressed I bonded with the three on my left and had a good laugh. It was uncomfortable however, and on the first night I only got a little sleep as I had to kip sitting upright. We were nearing the Yugoslav border when I woke, and had passed through by the time I was properly awake.

After travelling through countryside I remembered from nine months previously, we arrived in Zagreb at about 10 p.m. and several people disembarked, including the American couple. Although I was sorry to see them leave, there was also a positive side, as nobody took their places and there was more room for us. This made the journey more comfortable in the long term, but was outweighed in the short by a boy opening the back door and not being able to close it; meaning we had a cold draft in the back until the conductor fixed it two hours later. The woman sitting next to the boy slapped him, and he responded by attacking her; she was obviously ruffled by this, and disembarked at the next stop. I also had a bit of an argument with a man in front of me, as he was taking all my space and cramping my leg.

I woke briefly when we crossed into Austria at about 1 a.m. and then awakened properly at about 6 a.m. The bus journey terminated in Salzburg, and we got on a train for the final leg of the trip; the train fare was included in our ticket but Bernhard was heading to Zurich and took another route. It was a relief to get off the bus and onto a comfortable train, and Martin and I shared a roomy compartment.

The weather welcomed us with persistent rain, and the journey through lush green Western Europe on a wet Sunday morning reminded me of returning from the *Monsters of Rock* festival the week before I started travelling. Reminiscing about that weekend led me to think about what followed it, and as my adventure approached its conclusion I relived it in my mind. I'd exceeded my plans, seen some great places, met many wonderful people and had some terrific times. Yeh, it'd been grand, and I was glad I hadn't turned back after that soggy first day and night in Belgium!

The Guns N' Roses Worker-Traveller

The Hole in the Shack gang in Camping Nomentana, Rome

www.ingramcontent.com/pod-product-compliance
Lightning Source LLC
Chambersburg PA
CBHW022134080426
42734CB00006B/355